A PRISON CHAPLAIN'S MINISTRY

Behind Bars and Beyond

Dr. Maxwell Shimba

Copyright © 2024 – Dr. Maxwell Shimba

Shimba Publishing, LLC.

Printed in the United States of America

TABLE OF CONTENTS

INTRODUCTION

A Prison Chaplain's Ministry

Incarceration often signifies a period of immense struggle and transformation for individuals. Behind the high walls and barred windows, a world exists that is rarely seen by the public. This world is filled with stories of regret, redemption, despair, and hope. Amidst the complexities of prison life, there is a unique and profound ministry dedicated to providing spiritual care, guidance, and support to inmates. This is the ministry of prison chaplaincy.

"A Prison Chaplain's Ministry" by Dr. Maxwell Shimba offers an in-depth exploration of the vital role prison chaplains play within the correctional system. Dr. Shimba, an experienced chaplain and esteemed theologian, draws on years of firsthand experience and scholarly research to illuminate the multifaceted responsibilities and profound impact of this unique vocation.

The Essence of Prison Chaplaincy

Prison chaplains serve as spiritual guides, counselors, and advocates, providing a beacon of hope and compassion in an often harsh and unforgiving environment. Their work goes beyond the traditional boundaries of ministry, requiring a blend of theological knowledge, pastoral care, and practical skills to address the diverse needs of inmates. This book delves into the daily life of a prison chaplain, examining their various roles and the challenges they face.

A Journey Through the Book

The journey through "A Prison Chaplain's Ministry" begins with an overview of the chaplain's role, exploring how these spiritual leaders provide essential support to inmates. We then delve into the rich history of prison chaplaincy, tracing its evolution from its early roots to its present form within modern correctional systems. The book covers the rigorous training and preparation required to become a chaplain, highlighting the importance of theological education and pastoral training.

Readers will gain insight into the daily routines and diverse duties of chaplains, from conducting religious services to providing one-on-one counseling. The book addresses the spiritual needs of inmates, emphasizing the importance of inclusive care that respects diverse beliefs. It explores the critical role chaplains play in crisis intervention and counseling, offering support during times of violence, mental health crises, and personal tragedies.

Dr. Shimba also examines the chaplain's role in supporting rehabilitation and reintegration, leading programs that help inmates develop life skills, moral values, and a sense of purpose. The book emphasizes the importance of collaboration with prison staff, highlighting the dynamics of these relationships and the teamwork necessary to achieve the best outcomes for inmates.

Addressing Ethical and Moral Challenges

The ethical and moral challenges faced by prison chaplains are thoroughly examined, providing readers with an understanding of the complex dilemmas these spiritual leaders navigate. Real-life case studies and testimonials illustrate the transformative power of faith and spiritual support, showcasing the profound impact chaplains have on the lives of inmates.

The Broader Impact of Chaplaincy

"A Prison Chaplain's Ministry" also reviews evidence supporting the effectiveness of faith-based programs in reducing recidivism, demonstrating how prison chaplaincy contributes to long-term positive outcomes for inmates. The book highlights the importance of community outreach and support, showing how chaplains extend their ministry beyond the prison walls to engage with communities and support the families of inmates.

The personal growth and fulfillment experienced by chaplains in their vocation are explored, revealing the deep sense of purpose and spiritual development that comes with serving in this challenging environment. The book concludes with a look at future directions in prison chaplaincy, discussing emerging trends, the integration of technology, and new approaches to spiritual care.

A Call for Support and Recognition

Throughout the book, Dr. Shimba emphasizes the need for continued support and recognition of prison chaplaincy as an essential component of the criminal justice system. The dedication, compassion, and resilience of chaplains make a profound difference in the lives of inmates, fostering hope, healing, and positive change. By supporting and uplifting prison chaplains, we can contribute to a more just and humane prison system, promoting rehabilitation and successful reintegration for those who need it most.

Invitation to the Reader

As you embark on this journey through "A Prison Chaplain's Ministry," I invite you to open your heart and mind to the stories and insights shared within these pages. Whether you are a fellow chaplain, a member of the clergy, a corrections professional, or simply someone interested in the transformative power of faith and compassion, this book offers valuable perspectives on the vital work of prison chaplains. Together, let us recognize and celebrate the extraordinary ministry that brings light and hope into the darkest corners of our world.

Dr. Maxwell Shimba

Prison Chaplain

DR. MAXWELL SHIMBA

CHAPTER 01

THE UNIQUE ROLE OF A PRISON CHAPLAIN

The role of a prison chaplain is one that demands a profound commitment to faith, compassion, and understanding. Unlike other forms of ministry, prison chaplaincy places spiritual leaders in one of the most challenging environments imaginable, where they must navigate the complexities of the prison system, address the diverse needs of inmates, and often work within the constraints of limited resources and institutional regulations. This book aims to provide an in-depth exploration of the multifaceted responsibilities and experiences of prison chaplains, shedding light on their daily lives, the impact they have on the incarcerated, and the broader implications for society.

A Calling to Serve

For many prison chaplains, their work is more than a job—it is a calling. They are driven by a deep sense of purpose and a desire to make a difference in the lives of those who are often forgotten or marginalized. The prison environment is one where hope can be scarce, and the chaplain's presence can provide a crucial source of comfort and guidance. This chapter will explore what draws individuals to this unique form of ministry and the personal qualities and professional skills that make an effective prison chaplain.

The Evolution of Prison Chaplaincy

The history of prison chaplaincy dates back centuries, with roots in various religious traditions that emphasize the importance of caring for the marginalized and the imprisoned. Over time, the role has evolved, adapting to changes in the criminal justice system and societal attitudes towards incarceration. Today, prison chaplains come from diverse religious backgrounds and serve in a variety of correctional settings, from maximum-security prisons to juvenile detention centers. This section will provide a brief overview of the history and evolution of prison chaplaincy, highlighting key milestones and developments.

Daily Responsibilities

The daily life of a prison chaplain is varied and demanding. Chaplains are responsible for conducting religious services, providing spiritual and emotional support, offering crisis intervention, and facilitating educational and rehabilitative programs. They must be prepared to address the needs of inmates from a wide range of religious and cultural backgrounds, often working in an environment that can be volatile and unpredictable. This chapter will provide a glimpse into a typical day in the life of a prison chaplain, illustrating the range of activities and responsibilities they undertake.

Impact on Inmates

The presence of a prison chaplain can have a profound impact on the lives of inmates. For many, the chaplain provides a lifeline—a source of hope and support in an otherwise bleak environment. Through counseling, spiritual guidance, and various programs, chaplains help inmates cope with the challenges of prison life, address issues of guilt and remorse, and work toward rehabilitation and reintegration into society. This section will explore the ways in which chaplains make a difference in the lives of inmates, drawing on real-life stories and testimonials.

Broader Implications for Society

The work of prison chaplains extends beyond the prison walls, with broader implications for society as a whole. Effective chaplaincy can contribute to lower recidivism rates, improved mental health outcomes, and the successful reintegration of former inmates into their communities. By fostering an environment of hope and transformation, chaplains play a crucial role in the rehabilitation process and the promotion of restorative justice. This chapter will examine the societal benefits of prison chaplaincy, highlighting its importance in the broader context of the criminal justice system.

Challenges and Rewards

While the role of a prison chaplain is undoubtedly challenging, it is also deeply rewarding. Chaplains often face ethical dilemmas, limited resources, and the emotional toll of working in a high-stress environment. However, the opportunity to make a positive impact on the lives of inmates and contribute to their personal growth and rehabilitation provides a profound sense of fulfillment. This section will explore the challenges and rewards of prison chaplaincy, offering insights into what keeps chaplains motivated and committed to their calling.

The introduction chapter sets the stage for a comprehensive exploration of prison chaplaincy, providing an overview of the unique and multifaceted role chaplains play within the prison system. As we delve deeper into the subsequent chapters, we will uncover the various aspects of their ministry, the challenges they face, and the significant impact they have on inmates and society. Through this book, we aim to honor the dedication and compassion of prison chaplains and highlight the crucial role they play in fostering hope, healing, and transformation behind bars and beyond.

CHAPTER 02

THE ROLE OF A PRISON CHAPLAIN

Spiritual Guides

One of the primary roles of a prison chaplain is to serve as a spiritual guide for inmates. In a setting where despair and hopelessness can be pervasive, the chaplain's role is to offer spiritual nourishment and guidance. They conduct regular religious services, such as worship services, prayer meetings, and Bible studies, catering to the diverse religious needs of the inmate population. By facilitating these services, chaplains provide inmates with opportunities for reflection, repentance, and spiritual growth.

Chaplains also engage in one-on-one spiritual counseling, helping inmates to explore their faith, find meaning in their experiences, and develop a personal relationship with a higher power. This guidance can be particularly transformative for inmates struggling with guilt, shame, or a sense of purposelessness. Through spiritual mentorship, chaplains help inmates to find hope and resilience, even in the most challenging circumstances.

Counselors and Emotional Support

In addition to their spiritual duties, prison chaplains serve as counselors, providing crucial emotional support to inmates. The prison environment is often fraught with stress, anxiety, and emotional turmoil. Inmates may be dealing with a range of issues, including separation from loved ones, fear for their safety, and the emotional impact of their crimes and sentences.

Chaplains are trained to provide compassionate listening and empathetic support. They offer a safe and non-judgmental space for inmates to express their fears, frustrations, and regrets. This emotional support can be vital in helping inmates to manage their mental health and cope with the pressures of prison life.

Chaplains also provide crisis intervention, assisting inmates during times of acute distress, such as the loss of a loved one, personal conflict, or incidents of violence within the prison. They offer immediate support and guidance, helping inmates to navigate these crises and find a path forward.

Advocates for Inmates

Prison chaplains often act as advocates for inmates, working to ensure that their rights and needs are respected within the prison system. This advocacy can take many forms, from mediating conflicts between inmates and prison staff to addressing issues related to religious accommodation and access to spiritual resources.

Chaplains work to foster a more humane and just environment within the prison. They may intervene in cases where inmates are being mistreated or where their rights are being violated. By advocating for the dignity and well-being of inmates, chaplains help to promote a culture of respect and fairness within the correctional system.

Facilitators of Rehabilitation and Reintegration

A key aspect of the chaplain's role is to support the rehabilitation and reintegration of inmates. Chaplains lead and participate in various programs aimed at helping inmates to develop the skills and attitudes needed for successful reintegration into society. These programs may include educational classes, vocational training, substance abuse treatment, and anger management workshops.

Chaplains also facilitate restorative justice programs, which seek to repair the harm caused by criminal behavior through reconciliation and restitution. These programs provide inmates with opportunities to take responsibility for their actions, make amends, and develop a sense of empathy and accountability.

Through these efforts, chaplains play a crucial role in preparing inmates for life after prison. By addressing the root causes of criminal behavior and fostering personal growth, chaplains help inmates build a foundation for a more positive and productive future.

Navigating the Challenges of Prison Life

Prison life presents numerous challenges, both practical and existential. Chaplains help inmates to navigate these challenges, offering guidance and support on a wide range of issues. They may assist inmates in understanding and complying with prison rules and regulations, mediating conflicts, and finding ways to stay connected with their families and communities.

Chaplains also help inmates to find purpose and meaning in their daily lives. Through religious instruction, spiritual counseling, and various programs and activities, chaplains encourage inmates to engage in positive and constructive pursuits. This can include involvement in religious study groups, participation in community service projects, or the pursuit of educational and vocational goals.

The Significance of Chaplaincy Work

The work of prison chaplains is significant on multiple levels. For inmates, chaplains provide essential support that can make a profound difference in their lives. Through spiritual guidance, emotional support, advocacy, and rehabilitation programs, chaplains help inmates to cope with the challenges of incarceration and to find a path toward healing and transformation.

For the prison system as a whole, chaplains contribute to a more humane and just environment. Their presence helps to promote respect, compassion, and fairness, fostering a culture that supports the well-being and rehabilitation of inmates. Chaplains also play a key role in bridging the gap between the prison and the wider community, facilitating programs and initiatives that support reintegration and reduce recidivism.

In a broader societal context, the work of prison chaplains underscores the importance of compassion, redemption, and restorative justice. By supporting the spiritual and emotional needs of inmates, chaplains help to create a more just and compassionate society, one that recognizes the potential for growth and transformation in every individual.

Conclusion

The role of a prison chaplain is complex and multifaceted, encompassing spiritual guidance, emotional support, advocacy, and rehabilitation. Chaplains serve as beacons of hope and compassion in an often harsh and challenging environment, making a profound difference in the lives of inmates and the broader prison system. As we continue to explore the various aspects of prison chaplaincy in this book, we will gain a deeper understanding of the crucial work chaplains do and the impact they have on individuals and society.

CHAPTER 03

HISTORY AND EVOLUTION OF PRISON CHAPLAINCY

Early Roots in Religious Institutions

The concept of prison chaplaincy has deep historical roots, intertwined with the broader history of religion and social justice. The earliest forms of chaplaincy can be traced back to the medieval period, when religious orders and charitable organizations took on the responsibility of caring for the spiritual and physical needs of prisoners. Monastic orders, such as the Franciscans and Dominicans, played a crucial role in this early form of prison ministry, emphasizing the importance of compassion, mercy, and redemption.

During this time, prisons were often rudimentary and harsh, serving as places of punishment and penance. The presence of religious figures within these institutions provided a counterbalance to the punitive nature of the system, offering inmates spiritual solace and the hope of moral and personal transformation. Religious services, sacraments, and pastoral care became integral components of prison life, laying the groundwork for the formalization of prison chaplaincy.

The Enlightenment and Penal Reform

The Enlightenment period of the 18th century brought significant changes to the philosophy of punishment and the role of religion in the penal system. Enlightenment thinkers such as Cesare Beccaria and Jeremy Bentham advocated for a more rational and humane approach to punishment, emphasizing the potential for rehabilitation and the importance of moral and spiritual development.

This shift in thinking led to a wave of penal reforms across Europe and North America, with a growing recognition of the need for structured programs to support the rehabilitation of offenders. Religious leaders and organizations were at the forefront of these reforms, advocating for the establishment of chaplaincy programs within prisons. The Quakers, in particular, played a pivotal role in the development of modern prison chaplaincy, emphasizing the principles of penitence, reflection, and spiritual renewal.

In the United States, the establishment of the Pennsylvania System in the early 19th century marked a significant milestone in the evolution of prison chaplaincy. This system, characterized by solitary confinement and labor, included a strong emphasis on religious instruction and moral reform. Prison chaplains were appointed to provide spiritual guidance, conduct religious services, and offer educational programs, reflecting the growing belief in the transformative power of faith.

Institutionalization and Professionalization

The 19th and early 20th centuries saw the further institutionalization and professionalization of prison chaplaincy. As the prison system expanded and became more complex, the need for trained and dedicated chaplains became increasingly apparent. Religious denominations began to formalize the training and accreditation of prison chaplains, establishing specialized programs and institutions to prepare individuals for this unique form of ministry.

During this period, several key figures emerged who significantly shaped the field of prison chaplaincy. One notable figure was John Clay, the first chaplain appointed to the newly constructed Pentonville Prison in London in 1842. Clay's work emphasized the importance of education, moral instruction, and personal reform, setting a standard for prison chaplaincy that influenced subsequent generations.

In the United States, Louis Dwight, a Congregational minister, played a crucial role in the development of prison chaplaincy. As the founder of the Boston Prison Discipline Society in 1825, Dwight advocated for the appointment of chaplains in prisons and the implementation of moral and religious education programs. His efforts contributed to the widespread adoption of chaplaincy programs in American prisons.

The Modern Era

The mid-20th century marked a period of significant change and growth for prison chaplaincy. The post-World War II era saw a renewed emphasis on human rights, social justice, and the rehabilitation of offenders. These developments influenced the role of prison chaplains, who increasingly became advocates for the humane treatment of inmates and the promotion of restorative justice.

In many countries, the role of the prison chaplain expanded to include a broader range of responsibilities, such as counseling, crisis intervention, and the facilitation of educational and vocational programs. The establishment of professional associations, such as the American Correctional Chaplains Association (ACCA) and the International Prison Chaplains' Association (IPCA), provided a platform for chaplains to share best practices, receive ongoing training, and advocate for the importance of their work within the correctional system.

The modern era also saw a growing recognition of the need for interfaith chaplaincy, reflecting the increasing religious diversity of prison populations. Chaplains from various faith traditions began to work together to provide inclusive and respectful spiritual care, ensuring that the needs of all inmates were met.

Key Milestones and Figures

The history of prison chaplaincy is marked by several key milestones and influential figures who have shaped the field. Some of these include:

- The Establishment of the Pennsylvania System (1829): This system emphasized solitary confinement and labor, with a strong focus on religious instruction and moral reform, setting a precedent for the integration of chaplaincy in the prison system.

- John Clay (1842): Appointed as the first chaplain of Pentonville Prison in London, Clay's work emphasized education and personal reform, influencing the development of prison chaplaincy standards.

- Louis Dwight (1825): Founder of the Boston Prison Discipline Society, Dwight's advocacy for chaplaincy programs and moral education in prisons contributed to the widespread adoption of these initiatives in the United States.

- The Formation of the American Correctional Chaplains Association (1948): This organization provided a professional network for chaplains, promoting best practices and supporting the development of the field.

- Interfaith Chaplaincy Initiatives (Late 20th Century): Recognizing the growing religious diversity of prison populations, chaplains from various faith traditions began to collaborate, ensuring inclusive and respectful spiritual care for all inmates.

The history and evolution of prison chaplaincy reflect broader changes in society's attitudes toward punishment, rehabilitation, and the role of religion in the correctional system. From its early roots in religious institutions to its current form as a professional and inclusive ministry, prison chaplaincy has consistently emphasized the importance of compassion, moral reform, and spiritual growth. As we continue to explore the various aspects of prison chaplaincy in this book, we will gain a deeper appreciation for the vital work chaplains do and the enduring impact they have on the lives of inmates and the broader society.

CHAPTER 04

TRAINING AND PREPARATION

The path to becoming a prison chaplain is marked by a rigorous and comprehensive training process. This chapter explores the various educational and professional qualifications required, the specific courses and training programs available, and the ongoing development necessary to maintain effectiveness in this challenging role.

Theological Education

A solid foundation in theological education is crucial for anyone aspiring to become a prison chaplain. Most chaplains hold at least a bachelor's degree in theology, religious studies, or a related field. Many positions require a master's degree in divinity (M.Div.), pastoral studies, or a similar discipline. These programs typically cover a wide range of topics, including biblical studies, systematic theology, church history, and pastoral care.

Theological education provides future chaplains with a deep understanding of their faith tradition, equipping them with the knowledge and skills necessary to provide spiritual guidance and support to inmates. Courses in pastoral care and counseling are particularly important, as they prepare chaplains to address the complex emotional and psychological needs of the prison population.

Pastoral Training

In addition to formal theological education, aspiring prison chaplains must undergo extensive pastoral training. This training focuses on developing the practical skills needed to provide effective spiritual care in a correctional setting. It often includes supervised ministry experiences, such as internships or clinical pastoral education (CPE) programs.

Clinical Pastoral Education is a critical component of pastoral training for many chaplains. CPE programs provide hands-on experience in various ministry settings, including hospitals, hospices, and prisons. These programs emphasize self-reflection, interpersonal skills, and the ability to provide empathetic and effective pastoral care. Participants work under the supervision of experienced chaplains, receiving feedback and guidance to enhance their ministerial competence.

Specialized Courses in Corrections and Criminal Justice

Understanding the unique environment of the prison system is essential for effective chaplaincy. Many theological schools and seminaries offer specialized courses in corrections and criminal justice as part of their chaplaincy programs. These courses cover a range of topics, including the history and philosophy of punishment, the structure and function of the correctional system, and the psychological and social dynamics of incarceration.

Courses on criminal justice provide chaplains with a deeper understanding of the legal and institutional context in which they will work. They learn about the rights of inmates, the roles and responsibilities of correctional staff, and the policies and procedures that govern prison operations. This knowledge is crucial for navigating the complex and often bureaucratic environment of the prison system.

Certification and Accreditation

Most prison chaplaincy positions require certification or accreditation from a recognized professional organization. Certification ensures that chaplains meet specific standards of education, training, and professional competence. In the

United States, organizations such as the American Correctional Chaplains Association (ACCA) and the Association of Professional Chaplains (APC) offer certification programs for prison chaplains.

Certification typically requires a combination of formal education, supervised ministry experience, and successful completion of a certification exam. It may also involve continuing education requirements to ensure that chaplains stay current with developments in the field and maintain their professional skills.

Ongoing Professional Development

The role of a prison chaplain is dynamic and continually evolving, requiring ongoing professional development to stay effective. Chaplains must stay abreast of new developments in theology, pastoral care, and correctional practices. They often participate in workshops, conferences, and continuing education courses to enhance their knowledge and skills.

Professional development opportunities are available through various organizations and institutions. The ACCA and other professional associations offer regular training events, webinars, and conferences on topics relevant to prison chaplaincy. Many seminaries and theological schools also provide continuing education programs for chaplains and other ministry professionals.

Skills and Qualities of Effective Prison Chaplains

In addition to formal education and training, effective prison chaplains must possess a range of personal qualities and professional skills. These include:

- Empathy and Compassion: The ability to understand and share the feelings of others is crucial for providing effective spiritual and emotional support to inmates.

- Resilience and Emotional Stability: Working in a prison environment can be emotionally challenging. Chaplains must have the resilience to cope with stress and maintain their own emotional well-being.

- Strong Communication Skills: Effective communication is essential for building relationships with inmates, staff, and other stakeholders. Chaplains must be able to listen actively, convey empathy, and communicate clearly and respectfully.

- Cultural Competence: Prisons are diverse environments, with inmates from various cultural, religious, and socioeconomic backgrounds. Chaplains must be able to navigate this diversity and provide inclusive and respectful care.

- Ethical Integrity: Chaplains must adhere to high ethical standards, maintain confidentiality, respect the dignity of all individuals, and navigate complex ethical dilemmas with integrity.

Becoming a prison chaplain requires a comprehensive and multifaceted approach to training and preparation. From theological education and pastoral training to specialized courses in corrections and criminal justice, aspiring chaplains must develop a wide range of knowledge and skills. Certification and ongoing professional development ensure that chaplains maintain their competence and stay current with developments in the field. By cultivating empathy, resilience, and strong communication skills, prison chaplains can effectively navigate the challenges of their role and provide meaningful spiritual and emotional support to inmates. As we continue to explore the various aspects of prison chaplaincy in this book, we will gain a deeper appreciation for the dedication and preparation required to serve in this unique and vital ministry.

CHAPTER 05

DAILY LIFE AND DUTIES

The daily life of a prison chaplain is characterized by a wide array of tasks and responsibilities that require flexibility, compassion, and resilience. Each day presents unique challenges and opportunities to make a meaningful impact on the lives of inmates and the broader prison community. This chapter offers a detailed look into the routines and duties of a prison chaplain, highlighting the diverse aspects of their work, from conducting religious services to providing personal counseling and collaborating with prison staff.

Morning Routine

For many prison chaplains, the day begins early. Arriving at the prison before the inmates are fully active allows chaplains to prepare for the day ahead. This preparation often involves reviewing the day's schedule, setting up for religious services, and addressing any urgent needs or requests that have arisen overnight.

Briefing with Staff: A typical morning might start with a briefing session with prison staff, including correctional officers, healthcare providers, and administrators. These briefings help chaplains stay informed about any incidents, updates, or specific inmate needs that might affect their duties. This collaboration is crucial for ensuring that the chaplain's work is integrated effectively with the overall operations of the prison.

Conducting Religious Services

One of the central duties of a prison chaplain is to conduct religious services for inmates. These services can include regular worship services, prayer meetings, Bible studies, and special religious observances for various faith traditions.

Preparation: Preparing for these services involves selecting readings, preparing sermons or discussion topics, and setting up any necessary materials or spaces. Chaplains must be sensitive to the diverse religious backgrounds of inmates, ensuring that services are inclusive and respectful of all faiths.

Service Delivery: During the service, chaplains lead prayers, deliver sermons, and facilitate discussions. These gatherings provide inmates with a sense of community, spiritual nourishment, and an opportunity for reflection and growth. For many inmates, these services are a highlight of their week, offering a break from the routines and challenges of prison life.

One-on-One Counseling

Providing one-on-one counseling is a significant part of a chaplain's daily duties. Inmates often seek out chaplains to discuss personal issues, seek spiritual guidance, or find support during times of crisis.

Counseling Sessions: These sessions can cover a wide range of topics, from dealing with guilt and remorse to coping with anxiety, depression, and family issues. Chaplains offer a listening ear, provide empathetic support, and help inmates explore their feelings and find ways to cope with their challenges.

Crisis Intervention: Chaplains are often called upon to provide crisis intervention, offering immediate support to inmates experiencing acute distress. This can include dealing with the aftermath of violence, personal loss, or severe mental health crises. The ability to remain calm, provide comfort, and offer practical advice is crucial in these situations.

Coordinating with Prison Staff

Effective collaboration with prison staff is essential for a chaplain's work. Throughout the day, chaplains coordinate with various departments to ensure that inmates' spiritual and emotional needs are met.

Multidisciplinary Meetings: Chaplains often participate in multidisciplinary meetings, working alongside healthcare providers, mental health professionals, and social workers to discuss and develop comprehensive care plans for inmates. This teamwork is vital for addressing the complex needs of the prison population.

Conflict Mediation: Chaplains also play a role in mediating conflicts between inmates or between inmates and staff. Their neutral and compassionate presence can help de-escalate tensions and facilitate constructive dialogue, contributing to a safer and more harmonious prison environment.

Administrative Duties

In addition to their direct ministry work, chaplains have various administrative responsibilities. These tasks are essential for the smooth operation of chaplaincy services and include record-keeping, reporting, and planning.

Documentation: Chaplains maintain detailed records of their interactions with inmates, documenting counseling sessions, religious services, and any incidents or concerns. This documentation is crucial for continuity of care and for coordinating with other professionals.

Program Development: Developing and planning programs is another key administrative duty. Chaplains design and implement religious education classes, support groups, and rehabilitative programs that address the spiritual and emotional needs of inmates. This planning involves coordinating with external organizations, securing resources, and evaluating the effectiveness of these programs.

Evening Routine

As the day winds down, chaplains often use the evening to follow up on any unresolved issues, prepare for the next day's activities, and spend time in personal reflection and prayer.

Follow-Up: Following up with inmates who have had significant experiences or crises during the day is important to ensure ongoing support and care. This might involve brief check-ins or more extended sessions, depending on the situation.

Personal Reflection: Given the emotionally taxing nature of their work, it is crucial for chaplains to engage in personal reflection and self-care. This time allows them to process their experiences, seek spiritual renewal, and maintain their well-being.

The daily life of a prison chaplain is demanding and diverse, requiring a blend of spiritual guidance, emotional support, administrative skills, and collaborative effort. Each day brings new challenges and opportunities to make a meaningful impact on the lives of inmates. By conducting religious services, providing one-on-one counseling, coordinating with staff, and managing administrative duties, chaplains play a vital role in fostering a supportive and rehabilitative prison environment. As we continue to explore the various aspects of prison chaplaincy in this book, we will gain a deeper appreciation for the dedication and resilience required to serve effectively in this unique and vital ministry.

CHAPTER 06

ADDRESSING THE SPIRITUAL NEEDS OF INMATES

In a prison environment, inmates come from diverse religious and spiritual backgrounds, each with unique beliefs, practices, and needs. Prison chaplains play a crucial role in providing inclusive spiritual care, respecting these diverse beliefs, and fostering an environment of religious tolerance and understanding. This chapter delves into the methods and approaches chaplains use to address the spiritual needs of inmates effectively, ensuring that every individual receives the support and guidance they require.

Understanding Diverse Religious Beliefs

Prison chaplains must have a broad understanding of various religious traditions to cater to the spiritual needs of a diverse inmate population. This knowledge extends beyond their own faith tradition and includes awareness of the beliefs, practices, and rituals of other religions commonly represented in the prison population, such as Islam, Buddhism, Hinduism, Judaism, and indigenous spiritualities.

Educational Preparation: Many chaplains receive formal education and training in world religions as part of their theological studies. This education provides a foundational understanding of different faith traditions, preparing chaplains to engage respectfully and knowledgeably with inmates from various backgrounds.

Continual Learning: Chaplains must commit to lifelong learning, continually expanding their knowledge of different religions and staying informed about the spiritual needs and practices of the inmates they serve. This ongoing education can include attending workshops, reading religious texts, and engaging in interfaith dialogues.

Providing Inclusive Spiritual Care

Inclusive spiritual care means offering support and services that acknowledge and respect the diverse religious beliefs and practices of inmates. Chaplains achieve this by creating an environment where all inmates feel valued and supported, regardless of their faith tradition.

Interfaith Services: Some chaplains organize interfaith services and events that bring together inmates from different religious backgrounds. These services can include prayers, reflections, and discussions that emphasize common spiritual themes such as hope, forgiveness, and redemption.

Individualized Care: Chaplains provide one-on-one spiritual counseling tailored to the individual needs of inmates. This personalized approach allows chaplains to address specific religious questions, provide guidance on spiritual practices, and offer support during personal crises.

Resource Provision: Ensuring that inmates have access to religious resources is a critical part of inclusive care. Chaplains work to provide religious texts, prayer materials, and other spiritual resources for inmates of various faiths. They also facilitate access to special dietary requirements, religious attire, and other accommodations necessary for inmates to practice their faith.

Respecting Diverse Beliefs

Respect for diverse religious beliefs is fundamental to the role of a prison chaplain. Chaplains must demonstrate a deep respect for all faith traditions, fostering an environment of mutual respect and understanding among inmates.

Non-Judgmental Attitude: Chaplains approach their work with a non-judgmental attitude, recognizing the inherent dignity and worth of every individual. This attitude helps to build trust and rapport with inmates, encouraging them to seek spiritual support and guidance.

Cultural Sensitivity: Cultural sensitivity is essential for respecting the diverse backgrounds of inmates. Chaplains strive to understand the cultural contexts of different religious practices and ensure that their spiritual care is culturally appropriate and respectful.

Advocacy for Religious Rights: Chaplains advocate for the religious rights of inmates, working to ensure that their freedom to practice their faith is protected. This advocacy can involve negotiating with the prison administration to accommodate religious observances, dietary restrictions, and other practices.

Fostering Religious Tolerance and Understanding

One of the key roles of a prison chaplain is to promote religious tolerance and understanding within the prison community. This involves creating opportunities for inmates to learn about and appreciate different faith traditions, thereby reducing prejudice and fostering a sense of unity.

Interfaith Dialogue: Chaplains facilitate interfaith dialogues and discussions, providing a platform for inmates to share their beliefs and learn from one another. These dialogues can help to break down barriers, dispel misconceptions, and build a sense of mutual respect and understanding.

Educational Programs: Offering educational programs on different religions can enhance inmates' understanding of various faith traditions. Chaplains can organize lectures, discussion groups, and workshops that explore the beliefs, practices, and histories of different religions.

Conflict Resolution: In a diverse prison environment, religious differences can sometimes lead to conflicts. Chaplains play a vital role in mediating these conflicts, promoting peaceful resolution, and encouraging inmates to respect each other's beliefs.

Case Studies and Examples

To illustrate the practical application of these principles, this section presents several case studies and examples of how chaplains address the spiritual needs of inmates from diverse backgrounds.

Case Study 1: Interfaith Service for Peace: A chaplain organized an interfaith service focused on the theme of peace, bringing together inmates from different religious backgrounds. The service included prayers, readings, and reflections from various faith traditions, highlighting the common desire for peace and reconciliation. Inmates reported feeling a sense of unity and shared purpose, and the service fostered a more tolerant and understanding atmosphere within the prison.

Case Study 2: One-on-One Counseling for a Muslim Inmate: A Muslim inmate struggling with the isolation of prison life sought the guidance of a chaplain. The chaplain, knowledgeable about Islamic practices, provided spiritual counseling that respected the inmate's faith, offering support during Ramadan and helping to facilitate access to halal food. This personalized care helped the inmate to feel valued and supported, strengthening his faith and resilience.

Case Study 3: Educational Program on World Religions: To promote religious tolerance, a chaplain developed an educational program on world religions. The program included weekly sessions where inmates learned about different faith traditions, participated in discussions, and shared their own religious experiences. The program helped to reduce prejudices, build mutual respect, and foster a more inclusive prison community.

Addressing the spiritual needs of inmates in a diverse prison environment is a complex and multifaceted task. Prison chaplains must be equipped with a deep understanding of various religious traditions, a commitment to inclusive spiritual care, and the ability to foster an environment of respect and understanding. By providing personalized support, respecting diverse beliefs, and promoting religious tolerance, chaplains play a crucial role in the spiritual and emotional well-being of inmates. As we continue to explore the various aspects of prison chaplaincy in this book, we will gain a deeper appreciation for the dedication and skill required to serve effectively in this unique and vital ministry.

CHAPTER 07

CRISIS INTERVENTION AND COUNSELING

Prison life is often unpredictable and challenging, with crises arising from violence, mental health issues, personal tragedies, and the inherent stress of incarceration. Prison chaplains play a crucial role in crisis intervention, providing support and counseling to help inmates navigate these difficult situations. This chapter explores the various aspects of crisis intervention and counseling, highlighting the chaplain's role in offering immediate support, facilitating long-term healing, and promoting overall well-being among inmates.

Understanding Crisis Situations in Prison

Crisis situations in prison can take many forms, each requiring a specific response and approach from the chaplain. These situations include, but are not limited to:

- Violence: Incidents of physical altercations, assaults, and riots can create a volatile and dangerous environment for inmates and staff.

- Mental Health Crises: Inmates with mental health conditions may experience episodes of severe anxiety, depression, psychosis, or suicidal ideation.

- Personal Tragedies: News of a loved one's death, family issues, or legal setbacks can profoundly affect an inmate's emotional and psychological state.

- Self-Harm and Suicide Attempts: Inmates may engage in self-harming behaviors or attempt suicide due to the pressures and despair of prison life.

Immediate Crisis Intervention

When a crisis occurs, immediate intervention is crucial to stabilize the situation and provide support. Chaplains are often among the first responders in such scenarios, offering a calm and compassionate presence.

Assessment and Triage: The first step in crisis intervention is assessing the situation to determine the immediate needs of the affected inmate. Chaplains must quickly evaluate the severity of the crisis, the inmate's mental and emotional state, and any potential risks to their safety or the safety of others.

Providing Emotional Support: Offering immediate emotional support is essential during a crisis. Chaplains provide a listening ear, validate the inmate's feelings, and offer reassurance. Their presence can help de-escalate the situation and create a sense of safety and stability.

Coordinating with Staff: Effective crisis intervention requires collaboration with prison staff, including correctional officers, medical personnel, and mental health professionals. Chaplains work with these teams to ensure that the inmate receives the appropriate care and support.

Emergency Procedures: In cases of severe mental health crises or suicide attempts, chaplains may need to initiate emergency procedures, such as contacting mental health professionals, arranging for medical treatment, or placing the inmate in a safe environment to prevent self-harm.

Counseling and Long-Term Support

While immediate intervention is critical, ongoing counseling and support are necessary for long-term healing and recovery. Chaplains provide continuous care to help inmates cope with the aftermath of a crisis and work towards emotional and spiritual well-being.

Individual Counseling: One-on-one counseling sessions allow chaplains to address the specific needs of inmates who have experienced a crisis. These sessions provide a safe space for inmates to express their feelings, explore their thoughts, and develop coping strategies. Chaplains use various therapeutic techniques, such as cognitive-behavioral therapy, to help inmates process their experiences and build resilience.

Group Counseling: Group counseling sessions can be beneficial for inmates who have experienced similar crises. These sessions foster a sense of community and mutual support, allowing inmates to share their experiences, offer encouragement, and learn from one another. Chaplains facilitate these groups, guiding discussions and ensuring a respectful and supportive environment.

Spiritual Guidance: Spiritual counseling is a key component of the chaplain's role. Inmates often seek spiritual guidance to make sense of their experiences and find meaning and purpose in their lives. Chaplains help inmates explore their faith, engage in spiritual practices, and draw strength from their beliefs during difficult times.

Referrals and Resources: Chaplains may refer inmates to additional resources and support services, such as mental health professionals, social workers, or substance abuse programs. Coordinating with these services ensures that inmates receive comprehensive care that addresses all aspects of their well-being.

Addressing Specific Crisis Situations

Different types of crises require tailored approaches and interventions. This section explores how chaplains address some of the most common crisis situations in prison.

Violence and Trauma: Incidents of violence can leave inmates traumatized and fearful. Chaplains provide trauma-informed care, helping inmates process their experiences, manage their fears, and develop coping mechanisms. They also work to restore a sense of safety and stability within the prison community.

Mental Health Crises: Mental health crises require specialized care and intervention. Chaplains collaborate closely with mental health professionals to provide appropriate support and treatment. They offer ongoing counseling, monitor the inmate's well-being, and advocate for necessary mental health services.

Personal Tragedies: News of a loved one's death or other personal tragedies can be devastating for inmates. Chaplains provide compassionate support, helping inmates grieve and process their emotions. They may also assist with practical matters, such as arranging for communication with family members or facilitating participation in memorial services.

Self-Harm and Suicide Prevention: Preventing self-harm and suicide is a critical aspect of a chaplain's work. Chaplains identify inmates at risk, provide immediate support, and develop safety plans in collaboration with mental health professionals. They also offer ongoing counseling and support to address underlying issues and promote healing.

The Impact of Crisis Intervention

Effective crisis intervention and counseling have a profound impact on the well-being of inmates and the overall prison environment. By providing immediate support and long-term care, chaplains help inmates navigate crises, build resilience, and work toward recovery. This support fosters a more positive and stable prison community, reducing the likelihood of further crises and promoting a culture of care and compassion.

Personal Transformation: Inmates who receive effective crisis intervention and counseling often experience significant personal transformation. They develop healthier coping mechanisms, build stronger support networks, and find meaning and purpose in their lives. This transformation can lead to improved mental health, reduced recidivism, and successful reintegration into society.

Community Well-Being: The presence of chaplains and their work in crisis intervention contribute to the overall well-being of the prison community. By addressing crises promptly and effectively, chaplains help maintain a safer and more stable environment. Their work promotes mutual respect, understanding, and support among inmates and staff.

Crisis intervention and counseling are vital components of a prison chaplain's role. By providing immediate support, offering ongoing counseling, and addressing specific crisis situations, chaplains help inmates navigate the challenges of prison life and work towards healing and recovery. Their efforts contribute to the overall well-being of the prison community, fostering a culture of care, compassion, and resilience. As we continue to explore the various aspects of prison chaplaincy in this book, we will gain a deeper appreciation for the dedication and skill required to serve effectively in this unique and vital ministry.

CHAPTER 08

REHABILITATION AND REINTEGRATION

A primary objective of prison chaplaincy is to support the rehabilitation and reintegration of inmates into society. Chaplains play a crucial role in helping inmates develop the life skills, moral values, and sense of purpose necessary for successful reentry into their communities. This chapter explores the various programs and initiatives that chaplains lead, highlighting their impact on inmates' lives and their potential to reduce recidivism.

Understanding Rehabilitation and Reintegration

Rehabilitation involves the process of helping inmates develop the skills, behaviors, and attitudes necessary to lead productive and law-abiding lives. Reintegration focuses on the transition from incarceration back into the community, ensuring that inmates can successfully adapt and contribute positively to society. Chaplains address both aspects through a holistic approach that includes spiritual, emotional, and practical support.

Spiritual Programs

Spiritual programs are a cornerstone of chaplain-led rehabilitation efforts. These programs help inmates explore their faith, develop a moral compass, and find meaning and purpose in their lives.

Religious Services and Study Groups: Regular religious services and study groups provide inmates with opportunities to engage in worship, prayer, and religious education. These gatherings foster a sense of community and spiritual growth, helping inmates build a strong foundation for their rehabilitation.

Spiritual Counseling: One-on-one spiritual counseling sessions allow chaplains to address individual inmates' spiritual needs and concerns. Through personalized guidance, chaplains help inmates navigate their faith journeys, find inner peace, and develop a sense of accountability and responsibility.

Faith-Based Rehabilitation Programs: Many chaplains lead or facilitate faith-based rehabilitation programs that integrate spiritual teachings with practical life skills. These programs often include components such as moral development, character building, and ethical decision-making, all grounded in religious principles.

Education and vocational training are critical components of successful rehabilitation and reintegration. Chaplains often collaborate with educational and vocational programs to provide inmates with the skills needed for gainful employment and personal growth.

Basic Education: Chaplains support basic education initiatives, such as literacy classes, GED programs, and high school equivalency courses. These programs equip inmates with fundamental academic skills that are essential for employment and further education.

Vocational Training: Vocational training programs offer inmates practical skills and certifications in various trades, such as carpentry, plumbing, electrical work, and culinary arts. Chaplains help facilitate these programs, encouraging inmates to pursue training that aligns with their interests and career goals.

Life Skills Workshops: Life skills workshops cover a range of topics, including financial literacy, job readiness, communication skills, and time management. Chaplains lead or support these workshops, providing inmates with the tools they need to navigate daily life and employment successfully.

Moral and character development are integral to the rehabilitation process. Chaplains emphasize the importance of ethical behavior, personal integrity, and accountability.

Ethical Decision-Making: Chaplains lead programs that teach ethical decision-making, helping inmates understand the consequences of their actions and the importance of making morally sound choices. These programs often include discussions, role-playing, and case studies to illustrate ethical dilemmas and appropriate responses.

Character Building: Character-building programs focus on developing virtues such as honesty, respect, responsibility, and empathy. Through activities, discussions, and reflection, chaplains help inmates cultivate these virtues, fostering personal growth and positive behavior.

Restorative Justice Initiatives: Restorative justice initiatives emphasize accountability, reconciliation, and making amends for wrongdoing. Chaplains facilitate these programs, which often involve victim-offender dialogues, community service, and restitution efforts. These initiatives help inmates take responsibility for their actions and work towards repairing the harm they have caused.

Mentorship and Peer Support

Mentorship and peer support are valuable components of rehabilitation and reintegration. Chaplains play a key role in fostering these relationships, providing inmates with guidance and support from both peers and mentors.

Mentorship Programs: Chaplains often establish mentorship programs that pair inmates with mentors from the community or within the prison. These mentors provide guidance, encouragement, and support, helping inmates navigate the challenges of incarceration and prepare for reintegration.

Peer Support Groups: Peer support groups offer inmates the opportunity to share their experiences, challenges, and successes with others who are going through similar journeys. Chaplains facilitate these groups, creating a safe and supportive environment for inmates to learn from and support each other.

Family and Community Connections

Maintaining and strengthening family and community connections are crucial for successful reintegration. Chaplains help inmates build and sustain these relationships, recognizing their importance in providing support and stability.

Family Counseling and Support: Chaplains offer family counseling and support services, helping inmates and their families navigate the complexities of incarceration and reentry. These services may include family therapy, parenting classes, and communication workshops.

Community Engagement: Chaplains encourage inmates to engage with their communities through volunteer work, community service projects, and restorative justice initiatives. These activities help inmates build positive relationships with community members and demonstrate their commitment to making amends and contributing to society.

Reentry Planning: Effective reentry planning is essential for successful reintegration. Chaplains work with inmates to develop comprehensive reentry plans that include housing, employment, education, and support services. They also connect inmates with community resources and organizations that can provide ongoing support after release.

Measuring Success and Impact

Assessing the success and impact of rehabilitation and reintegration programs is essential for continuous improvement. Chaplains and prison administrators use various metrics and evaluations to measure outcomes and identify areas for enhancement.

Recidivism Rates: Reducing recidivism is a primary goal of rehabilitation and reintegration programs. Chaplains track recidivism rates among program participants, using this data to assess the effectiveness of their initiatives and identify successful strategies.

Inmate Feedback: Inmate feedback is a valuable source of information for evaluating programs. Chaplains gather feedback through surveys, interviews, and focus groups, using inmates' insights to refine and improve their programs.

Program Evaluations: Formal program evaluations, conducted by chaplains or external evaluators, provide a comprehensive assessment of the effectiveness and impact of rehabilitation initiatives. These evaluations consider various factors, including program participation, outcomes, and overall inmate well-being.

Rehabilitation and reintegration are central to the mission of prison chaplaincy. Through a holistic approach that includes spiritual programs, educational and vocational training, moral development, mentorship, and family and community connections, chaplains help inmates prepare for successful reentry into society. By addressing the diverse needs of inmates and providing comprehensive support, chaplains play a crucial role in reducing recidivism and promoting positive outcomes. As we continue to explore the various aspects of prison chaplaincy in this book, we will gain a deeper appreciation for the dedication and impact of chaplains in fostering rehabilitation and reintegration.

51

CHAPTER 09

COLLABORATION WITH PRISON STAFF

Effective prison chaplaincy hinges on close collaboration with a wide range of prison staff, including correctional officers, administrators, and healthcare professionals. These relationships are essential for creating a supportive environment that promotes the well-being and rehabilitation of inmates. This chapter examines the dynamics of these collaborative efforts, highlighting the importance of teamwork in achieving the best outcomes for inmates and the overall prison community.

Building strong, trusting relationships with prison staff is foundational for effective chaplaincy. These relationships are built on mutual respect, clear communication, and a shared commitment to the well-being of inmates.

Mutual Respect: Respecting the roles and responsibilities of correctional officers, administrators, and healthcare professionals is crucial. Chaplains must acknowledge the challenges and pressures faced by these staff members and appreciate their contributions to the prison environment.

Clear Communication: Open and clear communication is key to successful collaboration. Chaplains must regularly communicate with prison staff to share information, discuss inmate needs, and coordinate care. This communication can occur through formal meetings, informal conversations, and written reports.

Shared Goals: Identifying and working towards shared goals fosters a collaborative spirit. Chaplains and prison staff must recognize their common objective of promoting inmate rehabilitation, safety, and well-being. By aligning their efforts, they can create a more cohesive and supportive environment for inmates.

Roles and Responsibilities

Understanding the distinct roles and responsibilities of various prison staff members helps chaplains navigate their interactions and collaborations effectively.

Correctional Officers: Correctional officers are responsible for maintaining security, order, and discipline within the prison. They have direct daily contact with inmates and play a critical role in observing inmate behavior and identifying potential issues. Chaplains work closely with correctional officers to ensure that inmates' spiritual and emotional needs are addressed while maintaining security and order.

Administrators: Prison administrators oversee the overall operation of the facility, including policy development, staff management, and program implementation. They are instrumental in supporting chaplaincy programs and initiatives. Chaplains collaborate with administrators to secure resources, develop new programs, and address systemic issues affecting inmate care.

Healthcare Professionals: Healthcare professionals, including doctors, nurses, and mental health providers, deliver medical and mental health services to inmates. Chaplains often work alongside these professionals to provide holistic care that addresses both physical and emotional needs. This collaboration is especially important in cases involving mental health crises, chronic illnesses, or end-of-life care.

Collaborative Practices

Effective collaboration involves specific practices and strategies that enhance teamwork and communication among chaplains and prison staff.

Regular Meetings: Regular meetings with prison staff provide a structured opportunity to discuss inmate needs, program updates, and any emerging issues. These meetings can include multidisciplinary team meetings, case conferences, and informal check-ins.

Joint Training Programs: Joint training programs for chaplains and prison staff foster a shared understanding of each other's roles and responsibilities. These programs can cover topics such as crisis intervention, mental health awareness, conflict resolution, and cultural competence.

Integrated Care Plans: Developing integrated care plans that involve input from chaplains, healthcare providers, and correctional officers ensures that inmates receive comprehensive support. These plans address inmates' spiritual, emotional, and physical needs and outline specific interventions and follow-up actions.

Conflict Resolution: Addressing conflicts promptly and effectively is crucial for maintaining positive working relationships. Chaplains can play a mediating role in resolving conflicts between staff members or between staff and inmates. Open communication, empathy, and a focus on common goals are key to successful conflict resolution.

Challenges and Solutions

Collaboration with prison staff is not without challenges. Understanding these challenges and implementing effective solutions can enhance teamwork and improve outcomes.

Different Priorities: Chaplains and prison staff may have different priorities and perspectives. For example, while chaplains focus on spiritual care and rehabilitation, correctional officers prioritize security and order. Finding common ground and emphasizing shared goals can help bridge these differences.

Communication Barriers: Communication barriers, such as hierarchical structures or differing communication styles, can hinder collaboration. Establishing regular communication channels, such as scheduled meetings and clear reporting protocols, can mitigate these barriers.

Resource Limitations: Limited resources, including staffing, funding, and facilities, can impact the effectiveness of chaplaincy programs. Collaborating with administrators to advocate for necessary resources and exploring creative solutions, such as volunteer programs or partnerships with community organizations, can address these limitations.

Cultural Differences: Cultural differences between chaplains and prison staff, or among the staff themselves, can create misunderstandings and tension. Promoting cultural competence through training and education can enhance mutual understanding and respect.

Success Stories and Best Practices

Highlighting success stories and best practices provides valuable insights into effective collaboration between chaplains and prison staff.

Case Study 1: Mental Health Crisis Intervention: In one prison, chaplains and mental health professionals developed a collaborative crisis intervention program. Chaplains received training in mental health first aid, enabling them to provide immediate support during mental health crises. The program also included regular debriefing sessions with mental health staff, ensuring coordinated care and support for affected inmates. This collaboration resulted in improved outcomes for inmates experiencing mental health crises and strengthened relationships between chaplains and healthcare professionals.

Case Study 2: Reentry Planning Team: Another prison established a reentry planning team comprising chaplains, correctional officers, administrators, and community representatives. The team met regularly to develop individualized reentry plans for inmates, addressing their spiritual, educational, vocational, and housing needs. This holistic approach facilitated successful reintegration, reduced recidivism rates, and fostered a sense of shared purpose among team members.

Case Study 3: Cultural Competence Training: In a diverse prison setting, chaplains and prison staff participated in joint cultural competence training. The training included workshops on different religious and cultural practices, implicit bias, and effective communication. This initiative improved staff members' understanding and respect for inmates' diverse backgrounds, enhancing the overall prison environment and promoting better collaboration.

The Importance of Teamwork

Teamwork is at the heart of effective prison chaplaincy. By working together, chaplains and prison staff can create a more supportive and rehabilitative environment for inmates.

Shared Responsibility: Recognizing that the well-being and rehabilitation of inmates are shared responsibilities fosters a collaborative spirit. Chaplains and prison staff must view each other as partners in achieving common goals.

Mutual Support: Providing mutual support and encouragement strengthens the working relationship between chaplains and prison staff. Celebrating successes, acknowledging each other's contributions, and offering assistance during challenging times build a positive and cohesive team dynamic.

Continuous Improvement: Embracing a mindset of continuous improvement ensures that collaboration efforts evolve and adapt to meet the changing needs of inmates and the prison environment. Regular feedback, evaluation, and willingness to implement new strategies contribute to ongoing success.

Collaboration with prison staff is essential for effective prison chaplaincy. By building strong relationships, understanding roles and responsibilities, implementing collaborative practices, and addressing challenges, chaplains and prison staff can work together to achieve the best outcomes for inmates. This teamwork fosters a supportive and rehabilitative environment that promotes the well-being and successful reintegration of inmates. As we continue to explore the various aspects of prison chaplaincy in this book, we will gain a deeper appreciation for the critical role of collaboration in this unique and vital ministry.

CHAPTER 10

ETHICAL AND MORAL CHALLENGES

Prison chaplains often encounter complex ethical and moral challenges in their work, balancing their duty to support inmates with the harsh realities of the prison system. These challenges require chaplains to navigate difficult situations with wisdom, integrity, and a deep sense of compassion. This chapter delves into some of the most significant ethical and moral dilemmas faced by prison chaplains and offers insights into how they navigate these challenges.

Confidentiality vs. Safety

One of the most common ethical dilemmas for prison chaplains is the balance between maintaining confidentiality and ensuring safety. Inmates often confide in chaplains about personal issues, including thoughts of self-harm or plans for violence. While confidentiality is a cornerstone of pastoral care, chaplains must also consider the safety of the individual and others within the prison.

Maintaining Trust: Chaplains strive to create a safe and trusting environment where inmates feel comfortable sharing their thoughts and feelings. They emphasize the importance of confidentiality, explaining the boundaries and potential exceptions upfront.

Assessing Risk: When an inmate discloses information that poses a potential risk to themselves or others, chaplains must carefully assess the situation. They consider the immediacy and severity of the threat, the inmate's history, and the potential consequences of breaking confidentiality.

Taking Action: In cases where safety is at risk, chaplains may need to break confidentiality to prevent harm. This decision is never taken lightly and involves careful consideration and consultation with mental health professionals and prison staff. Chaplains explain their actions to the inmate, emphasizing their duty to protect everyone involved.

Dual Loyalty

Chaplains often experience dual loyalty, torn between their commitment to the inmates and their obligations to the prison administration. This can create ethical tensions, particularly when the goals of inmate care and institutional security conflict.

Balancing Roles: Chaplains balance their roles by maintaining clear professional boundaries and prioritizing the well-being of inmates within the constraints of the prison environment. They advocate for inmates' needs while respecting the rules and regulations of the institution.

Ethical Decision-Making: When faced with conflicting loyalties, chaplains rely on ethical decision-making frameworks. They consider the potential impact of their actions on all parties involved, consult with colleagues and supervisors, and reflect on their core values and professional standards.

Advocacy and Mediation: Chaplains often act as advocates and mediators, seeking solutions that address the concerns of both inmates and the administration. They work to find common ground and promote understanding and cooperation between all stakeholders.

Respecting Diverse Beliefs

Prison chaplains serve a diverse inmate population with varying religious beliefs and practices. Navigating this diversity ethically requires chaplains to respect and support all inmates, regardless of their faith tradition.

Inclusive Care: Chaplains provide inclusive spiritual care, ensuring that inmates of all faiths have access to religious services, resources, and support. They familiarize themselves with different religious practices and collaborate with representatives from various faith traditions.

Cultural Competence: Developing cultural competence is essential for respecting diverse beliefs. Chaplains engage in ongoing education and training to deepen their understanding of different cultures and religions, and they approach each inmate with empathy and openness.

Non-Proselytization: Ethical chaplaincy involves respecting inmates' religious choices without attempting to convert or influence them. Chaplains focus on providing support and guidance that aligns with the inmate's beliefs and spiritual needs.

Navigating Power Dynamics

The power dynamics within a prison environment can present ethical challenges for chaplains. Inmates may view chaplains as authority figures, which can influence their interactions and create potential conflicts of interest.

Maintaining Professional Boundaries: Chaplains maintain clear professional boundaries to navigate power dynamics ethically. They avoid favoritism, maintain impartiality, and ensure that their actions are guided by the best interests of the inmates.

Empowerment: Chaplains work to empower inmates, encouraging them to take an active role in their spiritual and personal development. They provide guidance and support while fostering a sense of autonomy and self-responsibility.

Self-Reflection: Regular self-reflection helps chaplains remain aware of their own biases and the impact of their position. They seek feedback from colleagues and supervisors and engage in continuous professional development to enhance their ethical practice.

Addressing Moral Distress

Moral distress arises when chaplains face situations that challenge their ethical and moral beliefs, such as witnessing injustice, dealing with institutional constraints, or feeling unable to provide adequate care.

Acknowledging Moral Distress: Recognizing and acknowledging moral distress is the first step in addressing it. Chaplains need to identify the sources of their distress and understand its impact on their well-being and professional practice.

Seeking Support: Chaplains can benefit from seeking support from colleagues, supervisors, and professional networks. Peer support groups, supervision sessions, and professional counseling can provide a safe space to discuss and process ethical dilemmas and moral distress.

Ethical Resilience: Developing ethical resilience involves building the capacity to navigate ethical challenges while maintaining one's moral integrity. Chaplains cultivate resilience through self-care, ongoing education, and reflective practice.

Case Studies and Examples

Examining real-life case studies and examples provides practical insights into how chaplains navigate ethical and moral challenges.

Case Study 1: Confidentiality vs. Safety: An inmate confides in a chaplain about their plans to harm another inmate. The chaplain faces the ethical dilemma of breaking confidentiality to prevent violence. After assessing the risk and consulting with mental health professionals, the chaplain decides to inform prison staff, emphasizing the duty to protect all individuals involved. The chaplain then works with the inmate to address the underlying issues and provide ongoing support.

Case Study 2: Dual Loyalty: A chaplain advocates for an inmate's need for religious accommodation, which conflicts with the prison's security protocols. The chaplain engages in ethical decision-making, consulting with both the inmate and the administration. By facilitating a dialogue and exploring alternative solutions, the chaplain helps find a compromise that respects the inmate's religious needs while maintaining institutional security.

Case Study 3: Respecting Diverse Beliefs: A chaplain encounters an inmate from a different faith tradition seeking spiritual guidance. The chaplain, unfamiliar with the inmate's beliefs, conducts research, consults with religious representatives, and provides support aligned with the inmate's faith. This approach demonstrates respect for diverse beliefs and fosters a positive spiritual environment.

Prison chaplains face a range of complex ethical and moral challenges in their work. By maintaining confidentiality while ensuring safety, balancing dual loyalties, respecting diverse beliefs, navigating power dynamics, and addressing moral distress, chaplains demonstrate ethical integrity and compassion. Through careful decision-making, ongoing education, and supportive collaboration, chaplains navigate these challenges effectively, fostering a rehabilitative and humane prison environment. As we continue to explore the various aspects of prison chaplaincy in this book, we gain a deeper appreciation for the ethical and moral resilience required to serve in this unique and vital ministry.

CHAPTER 11

CASE STUDIES AND TESTIMONIALS

Real-life case studies and testimonials provide a vivid picture of the impact of prison chaplaincy. These stories illustrate the transformative power of faith and spiritual support, offering insight into the profound changes that can occur in the lives of inmates through the dedicated work of chaplains. This chapter features personal accounts from chaplains and inmates, highlighting their journeys and the significant role that chaplaincy plays in fostering rehabilitation and hope.

Case Study 1: Redemption through Faith

Background: John, a long-term inmate serving a sentence for a violent crime, struggled with anger and remorse. Isolated and filled with despair, he had little hope for the future.

Chaplain's Role: Chaplain Sarah began visiting John regularly, offering spiritual counseling and emotional support. She introduced him to religious texts that spoke about forgiveness and redemption and encouraged him to join a Bible study group.

Transformation: Over time, John began to engage more deeply with his faith. He found solace in prayer and meditation, which helped him manage his anger. The support from Chaplain Sarah and the Bible study group gave him a sense of community and purpose. John's behavior improved, and he started mentoring younger inmates, sharing his story, and encouraging them to seek positive change.

Testimonial: "Chaplain Sarah showed me that my past didn't have to define my future. Through faith, I found forgiveness and a new sense of purpose. I now help others find their path, just as she helped me find mine."

Case Study 2: Overcoming Addiction

Background: Maria, an inmate with a history of substance abuse, faced numerous challenges during her incarceration. She struggled with withdrawal symptoms and the emotional pain that fueled her addiction.

Chaplain's Role: Chaplain David offered Maria spiritual counseling and introduced her to a faith-based recovery program. He provided her with religious texts and connected her with a support group of inmates dealing with similar issues.

Transformation: Maria's participation in the faith-based recovery program helped her develop coping mechanisms and a stronger sense of self-worth. The spiritual guidance and support from Chaplain David and the recovery group played a crucial role in her journey towards sobriety. Maria began leading prayer sessions and became an advocate for addiction recovery within the prison.

Testimonial: "Chaplain David and the recovery program gave me the tools I needed to overcome my addiction. Through faith, I've found the strength to stay sober and help others on their journey to recovery."

Case Study 3: Healing from Trauma

Background: James, a veteran serving a sentence for a violent offense, struggled with PTSD and depression. His traumatic experiences made it difficult for him to trust others and cope with prison life.

Chaplain's Role: Chaplain Karen, trained in trauma-informed care, provided James with specialized spiritual counseling. She introduced him to mindfulness practices and facilitated a veterans' support group within the prison.

Transformation: The spiritual counseling and mindfulness practices helped James manage his PTSD symptoms and regain a sense of control over his emotions. The veterans' support group provided a safe space for him to share his experiences and connect with others who understood his struggles. James began volunteering to assist new inmates with similar backgrounds, offering them support and guidance.

Testimonial: "Chaplain Karen helped me navigate my trauma and find peace through mindfulness and faith. The support group gave me a sense of belonging and purpose. Now, I'm able to help others heal, just as she helped me."

Case Study 4: Reconnecting with Family

Background: Emily, a mother serving a sentence for a non-violent offense, was estranged from her family. The separation from her children caused her immense grief and guilt.

Chaplain's Role: Chaplain Michael provided Emily with emotional and spiritual support, encouraging her to reconnect with her faith. He facilitated communication between Emily and her family, offering counseling sessions to address the underlying issues.

Transformation: Through Chaplain Michael's guidance, Emily found the courage to reach out to her family. The counseling sessions helped rebuild trust and communication, leading to reconciliation with her children.

Emily's renewed faith gave her the strength to focus on her rehabilitation and future reunification with her family.

Testimonial: "Chaplain Michael helped me reconnect with my faith and my family. His support and guidance were instrumental in healing the rift between me and my children. I now have hope for the future and a renewed commitment to being the best mother I can be."

Case Study 5: Embracing Diversity

Background: Ahmed, an inmate practicing Islam, felt isolated due to the lack of religious support for his faith tradition. He faced discrimination and struggled to maintain his religious practices.

Chaplain's Role: Chaplain Lisa, committed to inclusivity, worked to ensure that inmates of all faiths received appropriate spiritual support. She arranged for Ahmed to have access to religious texts, and prayer materials, and facilitated the observance of Islamic holidays.

Transformation: With Chaplain Lisa's support, Ahmed was able to practice his faith more fully. The inclusive environment fostered by Chaplain Lisa helped reduce discrimination and promoted understanding among inmates of different faiths. Ahmed began leading prayer sessions and educational programs about Islam, contributing to a more inclusive and respectful prison community.

Testimonial: "Chaplain Lisa's dedication to inclusivity allowed me to practice my faith and share it with others. Her support made a significant difference in my prison experience, fostering respect and understanding among inmates."

Chaplain Testimonials

Chaplain Sarah: "Seeing the transformation in inmates like John is what drives me. Witnessing their journey from despair to hope through faith is incredibly rewarding. It's a testament to the power of spiritual support and the resilience of the human spirit."

Chaplain David: "Helping inmates overcome addiction and find strength in their faith is a profound experience. It's about providing them with the tools and support they need to change their lives. Their success stories inspire me every day."

Chaplain Karen: "Working with trauma-affected inmates like James has shown me the importance of specialized care and understanding. The healing process is a journey, and being part of that journey is a privilege and a responsibility I hold dear."

Chaplain Michael: "Reconnecting families and providing emotional support to inmates like Emily is a vital part of my work. It's about restoring relationships and offering hope for a better future. The positive changes I see in these families reaffirm the importance of chaplaincy."

Chaplain Lisa: "Fostering inclusivity and supporting inmates of diverse faiths, like Ahmed, is central to my mission. Promoting understanding and respect among inmates creates a more harmonious and supportive prison environment. It's incredibly fulfilling to see the impact of this work."

The case studies and testimonials presented in this chapter highlight the transformative power of prison chaplaincy. Through spiritual support, emotional counseling, and inclusive care, chaplains play a vital role in helping inmates navigate their challenges, find hope, and work toward rehabilitation and reintegration. These stories serve as a testament to the profound impact of faith and compassion in the prison environment, illustrating the essential role chaplains play in fostering positive change and supporting the well-being of inmates. As we continue to explore the various aspects of prison chaplaincy in this book, we gain a deeper appreciation for the dedication and resilience required to serve in this unique and vital ministry.

CHAPTER 12

THE IMPACT OF FAITH ON RECIDIVISM

Recidivism, the tendency of previously incarcerated individuals to re-offend and return to prison, is a significant challenge for the criminal justice system. Research suggests that faith-based programs can play a crucial role in reducing recidivism rates. This chapter reviews the evidence supporting the effectiveness of these programs and explores how prison chaplaincy contributes to long-term positive outcomes for inmates.

Understanding Recidivism

Recidivism is a complex issue influenced by various factors, including socioeconomic conditions, lack of education and employment opportunities, substance abuse, and mental health issues. Effective rehabilitation and reintegration programs aim to address these underlying issues, providing inmates with the tools and support necessary to build stable, law-abiding lives upon release.

The Role of Faith-Based Programs

Faith-based programs, often facilitated by prison chaplains, focus on spiritual growth, moral development, and the cultivation of positive behaviors and attitudes. These programs offer inmates a sense of purpose, community, and hope, which are essential for successful rehabilitation and reintegration.

Key Components of Faith-Based Programs:

- Spiritual Counseling: One-on-one spiritual counseling sessions help inmates explore their faith, develop moral values, and find meaning and purpose in their lives.

- Religious Services and Study Groups: Regular participation in religious services and study groups fosters a sense of community and spiritual growth.

- Moral and Ethical Education: Programs that emphasize ethical decision-making, personal responsibility, and character development help inmates develop a moral compass.

- Support Networks: Faith-based programs often create strong support networks, including mentors and peer support groups, which provide ongoing encouragement and accountability.

Evidence Supporting Faith-Based Programs

Numerous studies have demonstrated the positive impact of faith-based programs on reducing recidivism rates. These programs have been shown to address several key factors that contribute to reoffending, including:

- Behavioral Change: Faith-based programs promote positive behavioral change by instilling moral values and encouraging ethical decision-making.

- Emotional and Psychological Support: Spiritual counseling and community support help inmates manage stress, cope with emotional challenges, and develop resilience.

- Social Integration: Participation in faith-based programs fosters a sense of belonging and community, reducing feelings of isolation and marginalization.

- Substance Abuse Recovery: Many faith-based programs include components focused on substance abuse recovery, providing inmates with the tools and support needed to overcome addiction.

Research Findings:

- Study by the Bureau of Justice Assistance: A study conducted by the Bureau of Justice Assistance found that inmates who participated in faith-based programs had significantly lower recidivism rates compared to those who did not participate.

- Florida Department of Corrections Study: Research by the Florida Department of Corrections revealed that inmates who completed faith-based programs were less likely to re-offend within three years of release.

- Meta-Analysis by Johnson and Larson: A meta-analysis by Byron Johnson and David Larson reviewed multiple studies and concluded that faith-based programs are effective in reducing recidivism, particularly when combined with other rehabilitative services.

How Prison Chaplaincy Contributes to Positive Outcomes

Prison chaplains play a vital role in facilitating faith-based programs and supporting inmates' spiritual and emotional needs. Their work significantly contributes to the long-term positive outcomes for inmates in several ways:

Spiritual Growth and Moral Development:

Chaplains help inmates develop a strong spiritual foundation and moral compass. Through spiritual counseling, religious services, and moral education, chaplains guide inmates in exploring their faith, understanding ethical principles, and making positive life choices.

Emotional and Psychological Support:

Chaplains provide crucial emotional and psychological support, helping inmates navigate the challenges of prison life and address underlying issues such as trauma, addiction, and mental health disorders. This support is essential for inmates' overall well-being and rehabilitation.

Building Support Networks:

Chaplains facilitate the creation of support networks, including mentors, peer support groups, and connections with faith communities outside the prison. These networks provide ongoing encouragement, accountability, and resources that are vital for successful reintegration.

Promoting Positive Behavior:

Through their work, chaplains promote positive behavior and attitudes among inmates. They encourage inmates to engage in constructive activities, such as education, vocational training, and community service, which contribute to personal growth and reduce the likelihood of reoffending.

Advocacy and Reintegration Support:

Chaplains often advocate for inmates' needs and support their reintegration efforts. They help inmates develop reentry plans, connect with community resources, and address barriers to successful reintegration, such as housing and employment challenges.

Case Studies and Success Stories

Examining specific case studies and success stories provides insight into the impact of faith-based programs and chaplaincy on reducing recidivism.

Case Study 1: The InnerChange Freedom Initiative (IFI):

The InnerChange Freedom Initiative, a faith-based program implemented in several states, including Texas, has demonstrated significant success in reducing recidivism rates. The program combines spiritual counseling, education, vocational training, and community support. Research indicates that participants in IFI are less likely to reoffend and more likely to find employment and stable housing after release.

Success Story: Michael's Journey:

Michael, an inmate with a history of substance abuse and repeated incarcerations, participated in a faith-based recovery program facilitated by Chaplain David. Through spiritual counseling, support groups, and vocational training, Michael found the strength to overcome his addiction and develop a positive outlook on life. After his release, he secured a job and became an active member of his faith community, successfully breaking the cycle of recidivism.

Case Study 2: The Kairos Prison Ministry:

The Kairos Prison Ministry offers weekend retreats and ongoing support groups for inmates, focusing on spiritual growth and community building. Studies have shown that participants in Kairos programs exhibit lower recidivism rates and improved behavior during incarceration. The program's emphasis on forgiveness, accountability, and personal transformation has led to positive outcomes for many inmates.

Success Story: Sarah's Transformation:

Sarah, an inmate serving a long sentence, participated in the Kairos Prison Ministry weekend retreat. The experience deeply impacted her, leading to a renewed faith and commitment to positive change. With ongoing support from the Kairos community and Chaplain Lisa, Sarah became a mentor to other inmates, helping them navigate their spiritual journeys and prepare for reintegration.

Challenges and Considerations

While faith-based programs and chaplaincy have demonstrated significant success in reducing recidivism, there are challenges and considerations to address:

- Program Accessibility: Ensuring that all inmates have access to faith-based programs and chaplaincy services is crucial. Efforts must be made to accommodate diverse religious beliefs and provide inclusive support.

- Quality and Consistency: The effectiveness of faith-based programs can vary depending on the quality of implementation and the consistency of support. Establishing standards and best practices can help maintain program effectiveness.

- Collaboration with Secular Programs: Integrating faith-based programs with secular rehabilitation services can enhance overall outcomes. Collaboration between chaplains, educators, mental health professionals, and social workers is essential for comprehensive inmate care.

Faith-based programs and prison chaplaincy play a vital role in reducing recidivism and promoting positive outcomes for inmates. Through spiritual growth, moral development, emotional support, and strong support networks, chaplains help inmates build the foundation for successful rehabilitation and reintegration. The evidence and case studies presented in this chapter highlight the transformative impact of faith and the essential role of chaplains in fostering hope and positive change within the prison system. As we continue to explore the various aspects of prison chaplaincy in this book, we gain a deeper appreciation for the profound and lasting impact of this unique and vital ministry.

CHAPTER 13

COMMUNITY OUTREACH AND SUPPORT

The work of prison chaplains does not end at the prison gates. Extending their ministry beyond the walls, chaplains engage with communities and provide vital support to the families of inmates. This chapter highlights the importance of community outreach and the pivotal role of chaplains in fostering positive connections between inmates, their families, and the wider community.

The Importance of Community Outreach

Community outreach is essential for the successful reintegration of inmates and the overall well-being of their families. By bridging the gap between the prison and the community, chaplains help create a supportive environment that facilitates rehabilitation and reduces recidivism.

Reintegration Support: Effective community outreach provides inmates with the resources and support they need to transition smoothly back into society. This includes assistance with housing, employment, education, and access to healthcare and social services.

Family Reunification: Strong family ties are crucial for the emotional and psychological well-being of inmates. Chaplains work to maintain and strengthen these connections, facilitating communication and providing counseling and support to both inmates and their families.

Community Education: Educating the community about the challenges faced by inmates and the importance of rehabilitation fosters a more supportive and understanding environment. Chaplains play a key role in raising awareness and promoting restorative justice principles.

Supporting Families of Inmates

The families of inmates often face significant emotional, financial, and social challenges. Chaplains provide vital support to these families, helping them navigate the complexities of having a loved one in prison.

Emotional Support: Families of inmates experience a range of emotions, including shame, guilt, anger, and sadness. Chaplains offer empathetic listening, counseling, and spiritual support to help families cope with these feelings and maintain hope.

Counseling Services: Chaplains provide individual and group counseling sessions for families, addressing issues such as communication, forgiveness, and relationship rebuilding. These services help families process their emotions and develop healthy coping strategies.

Practical Assistance: Families often need practical assistance, such as help with navigating the legal system, accessing social services, or managing financial difficulties. Chaplains connect families with community resources and provide guidance on available support programs.

Family Events: Organizing family events, such as visitation days, family reunification programs, and holiday celebrations, helps strengthen family bonds. Chaplains facilitate these events, creating opportunities for meaningful interactions between inmates and their families.

Building Community Partnerships

Collaborating with community organizations and faith-based groups enhances the support network available to inmates and their families. Chaplains play a crucial role in building these partnerships and coordinating efforts to provide comprehensive care.

Faith-Based Organizations: Many faith-based organizations offer programs and services that align with the goals of prison chaplaincy. Chaplains partner with these organizations to provide spiritual support, mentoring, and practical assistance to inmates and their families.

Social Service Agencies: Social service agencies offer a range of support services, including housing assistance, employment programs, substance abuse treatment, and mental health counseling. Chaplains connect inmates and their families with these agencies, ensuring they receive the help they need.

Educational Institutions: Collaborating with educational institutions provides inmates with access to educational opportunities and vocational training. Chaplains work with schools, colleges, and training centers to facilitate programs that enhance inmates' skills and employability.

Community Volunteers: Engaging community volunteers in outreach efforts expands the support network available to inmates and their families. Chaplains recruit and train volunteers to provide mentoring, tutoring, and other forms of assistance.

Case Studies and Success Stories

Real-life case studies and success stories illustrate the impact of community outreach and support on the lives of inmates and their families.

Case Study 1: Family Reunification Program

Background: The Family Reunification Program, led by Chaplain Emma, aimed to strengthen the bonds between inmates and their families. The program included counseling sessions, family visits, and special events designed to facilitate communication and healing.

Success Story: Through the program, inmate Carlos reconnected with his estranged wife and children. The counseling sessions helped them address past conflicts and rebuild trust. Family visits and events provided opportunities for positive interactions, leading to a renewed sense of unity and support. After his release, Carlos successfully reintegrated into his family, finding stable employment and maintaining a close relationship with his loved ones.

Testimonial: "The Family Reunification Program gave me a second chance with my family. Chaplain Emma's support and the program's activities helped us heal and rebuild our relationships. I couldn't have done it without their help."

Case Study 2: Community Mentorship Initiative

Background: The Community Mentorship Initiative, coordinated by Chaplain James, connected inmates with mentors from the local community. The mentors provided guidance, support, and encouragement, helping inmates prepare for life after release.

Success Story: Inmate Lisa participated in the mentorship initiative, where she was paired with Sarah, a community volunteer with experience in substance abuse recovery. Through regular meetings and support, Sarah helped Lisa develop coping strategies, set goals, and stay committed to her recovery. After her release, Lisa continued to receive support from Sarah and successfully maintained her sobriety, found employment, and became an advocate for others struggling with addiction.

Testimonial: "Having a mentor like Sarah made all the difference. Her guidance and support kept me on track and gave me hope for the future. The mentorship program changed my life."

Case Study 3: Educational Partnership Program

Background: Chaplain Robert partnered with a local college to offer educational programs to inmates. The partnership provided inmates with access to academic courses, vocational training, and career counseling.

Success Story: Inmate Marcus enrolled in the college's vocational training program, where he gained skills in carpentry and welding. With Chaplain Robert's encouragement and the college's resources, Marcus excelled in the program and earned several certifications. After his release, Marcus secured a job in construction and continued his education, working towards a degree in engineering.

Testimonial: "The educational program gave me a future I never thought possible. Chaplain Robert's support and the opportunities provided by the college helped me turn my life around. I'm now building a better life for myself and my family."

The Role of Chaplains in Community Outreach

Chaplains play a multifaceted role in community outreach, acting as facilitators, advocates, and connectors. Their efforts extend beyond the prison walls, creating a network of support that fosters rehabilitation and reintegration.

Facilitators: Chaplains organize and lead outreach programs, ensuring they are accessible and effective for inmates and their families. They coordinate logistics, recruit volunteers, and manage partnerships with community organizations.

Advocates: Chaplains advocate for the needs of inmates and their families, raising awareness about the challenges they face and promoting the importance of rehabilitation and reintegration. They work to change public perceptions and support policies that facilitate successful reentry.

Connectors: Chaplains connect inmates and their families with resources and support services, building bridges between the prison and the community. They ensure that inmates have access to the help they need, both during incarceration and after release.

Challenges and Considerations

While community outreach and support are essential, they come with challenges that chaplains must navigate.

Resource Limitations: Limited funding and resources can constrain the scope and effectiveness of outreach programs. Chaplains must be resourceful, seeking grants, donations, and volunteer support to sustain their efforts.

Stigma and Discrimination: Inmates and their families often face stigma and discrimination, which can hinder their reintegration efforts. Chaplains work to combat these negative perceptions through education and advocacy.

Coordination and Collaboration: Effective community outreach requires coordination and collaboration among various stakeholders. Chaplains must navigate complex networks and build strong partnerships to provide comprehensive support.

Sustainability: Ensuring the sustainability of outreach programs is crucial for long-term success. Chaplains focus on developing programs that can continue to operate and evolve, even as leadership and resources change.

Community outreach and support are vital components of prison chaplaincy, extending the ministry's impact beyond the prison walls. Through their efforts, chaplains foster positive connections between inmates, their families, and the wider community, promoting successful rehabilitation and reintegration. The case studies and success stories presented in this chapter highlight the transformative power of community outreach and the essential role of chaplains in this process. As we continue to explore the various aspects of prison chaplaincy in this book, we gain a deeper appreciation for the dedication and impact of chaplains in fostering hope and positive change both inside and outside the prison system.

CHAPTER 14

PERSONAL GROWTH AND FULFILLMENT

Serving as a prison chaplain is a vocation that offers profound opportunities for personal growth and spiritual development. While the role comes with significant challenges, it also provides deep personal rewards that can be transformative for both the chaplains and the inmates they serve. This chapter explores the personal journey of prison chaplains, highlighting the rewards, challenges, and overall fulfillment that comes with this unique ministry.

The Rewards of Prison Chaplaincy

Spiritual Fulfillment: One of the most significant rewards of prison chaplaincy is the deep sense of spiritual fulfillment. Chaplains often find that their faith is strengthened and deepened through their work with inmates. Engaging in daily prayer, offering spiritual guidance, and witnessing the transformative power of faith in the lives of inmates can lead to profound spiritual growth.

Making a Difference: Chaplains have the opportunity to make a tangible difference in the lives of inmates. Helping someone find hope, purpose, and direction can be incredibly rewarding. Knowing that their efforts contribute to the rehabilitation and reintegration of inmates provides chaplains with a strong sense of purpose and accomplishment.

Personal Relationships: Building meaningful relationships with inmates and their families is another rewarding aspect of prison chaplaincy. These connections often transcend the prison walls, creating lasting bonds based on trust, respect, and mutual support. Chaplains frequently hear from former inmates who attribute their successful reintegration to the support and guidance they received.

Witnessing Transformation: Seeing inmates transform their lives through faith and personal development is one of the most fulfilling aspects of being a prison chaplain. Witnessing an inmate go from despair to hope, from anger to peace, and from isolation to community is a powerful testament to the impact of chaplaincy.

Professional Growth: The role of a prison chaplain involves continuous learning and professional development. Chaplains acquire new skills in counseling, conflict resolution, and crisis intervention, which are valuable in both professional and personal contexts. This ongoing growth enhances their ability to serve effectively and adapt to the ever-changing needs of the prison environment.

The Challenges of Prison Chaplaincy

Emotional Toll: Working in a prison environment can be emotionally taxing. Chaplains are often exposed to the harsh realities of prison life, including violence, trauma, and suffering. Providing support to inmates who have experienced significant hardship can lead to emotional exhaustion and burnout if not managed properly.

Ethical Dilemmas: Chaplains frequently face complex ethical dilemmas, such as balancing confidentiality with safety, navigating dual loyalties between inmates and prison administration, and respecting diverse religious beliefs. These dilemmas require careful consideration, reflection, and sometimes difficult decision-making.

Resource Limitations: Limited resources and funding can hinder the effectiveness of chaplaincy programs. Chaplains often have to be resourceful and creative in finding ways to provide necessary support and services with constrained budgets and limited staff.

Navigating Power Dynamics: The power dynamics within a prison can be challenging to navigate. Chaplains must maintain professional boundaries while building trust and rapport with inmates and staff. Balancing these relationships requires sensitivity, empathy, and strong interpersonal skills.

Stigma and Misunderstanding: Prison chaplains sometimes face stigma and misunderstanding from the broader community. Their work is often underappreciated or misunderstood, which can be discouraging. Advocating for the importance of chaplaincy and educating others about its impact is an ongoing challenge.

Personal Growth through Challenges

Despite the challenges, many chaplains find that these difficulties contribute to their personal growth and development. Facing and overcoming obstacles can lead to increased resilience, empathy, and self-awareness.

Resilience: The ability to navigate and withstand the emotional and ethical challenges of prison chaplaincy builds resilience. Chaplains learn to cope with stress, manage their emotions, and find strength in their faith and professional support networks.

Empathy: Engaging with inmates and their families fosters a deep sense of empathy. Chaplains develop a greater understanding of the human condition, the impact of trauma, and the capacity for change and redemption. This empathy extends beyond the prison, enriching their interactions and relationships in all areas of life.

Self-Awareness: The reflective nature of chaplaincy work enhances self-awareness. Chaplains constantly evaluate their motivations, biases, and actions, leading to personal growth and a deeper understanding of themselves and their faith.

Spiritual Development: The spiritual journey of a prison chaplain is one of continual growth. The daily practice of prayer, meditation, and spiritual guidance deepens their faith and connection to their beliefs. This spiritual development is both a source of strength and a guiding light in their work.

Stories of Personal Fulfillment

Chaplain Anna's Journey: Anna, a prison chaplain for over a decade, found her calling in ministering to female inmates. Despite the emotional toll, she found deep fulfillment in helping women rediscover their faith and rebuild their lives. Anna's own faith grew stronger as she witnessed the transformative power of spiritual support. She shared, "Each time I see an inmate turn her life around, it reaffirms my belief in the resilience of the human spirit and the power of faith."

Chaplain Ben's Experience: Ben, who served as a chaplain in a maximum-security prison, faced numerous challenges, including navigating gang dynamics and addressing severe mental health issues. Through these experiences, Ben developed a profound sense of empathy and resilience. He stated, "The work is tough, but knowing that I've helped even one person find hope and change their path makes it all worthwhile."

Chaplain Maria's Story: Maria, a chaplain working in a juvenile detention center, found personal growth in mentoring young offenders. She focused on providing a stable, nurturing presence and teaching life skills through faith-based programs. Maria reflected, "Seeing these young people realize their potential and make positive changes is incredibly rewarding. It's a constant reminder of the impact we can have when we show love and compassion."

Strategies for Personal Growth and Fulfillment

Self-Care: Practicing self-care is essential for maintaining emotional and physical well-being. Chaplains should prioritize activities that rejuvenate them, such as exercise, hobbies, spending time with loved ones, and regular spiritual practice.

Professional Support: Engaging in professional support networks, supervision, and peer support groups provides chaplains with a space to share experiences, seek advice, and receive emotional support. This network is crucial for coping with the challenges of the role.

Continuing Education: Pursuing continuing education opportunities, such as workshops, courses, and conferences, helps chaplains stay informed about best practices and new developments in chaplaincy and related fields. Lifelong learning contributes to professional growth and enhances the quality of care provided.

Reflective Practice: Regular reflective practice, such as journaling, meditation, and prayer, helps chaplains process their experiences, gain insights, and maintain a connection to their faith. Reflection fosters self-awareness and personal growth.

Advocacy and Outreach: Chaplains can find fulfillment in advocating for the needs of inmates and educating the broader community about the importance of rehabilitation and restorative justice. Engaging in outreach efforts provides a sense of purpose and extends the impact of their work.

Serving as a prison chaplain is a deeply fulfilling vocation that offers significant opportunities for personal growth and spiritual development. While the role comes with challenges, the rewards of making a difference in the lives of inmates, witnessing transformation, and experiencing spiritual fulfillment are profound. Through self-care, professional support, continuing education, reflective practice, and advocacy, chaplains can navigate the challenges and find lasting fulfillment in their ministry. As we continue to explore the various aspects of prison chaplaincy in this book, we gain a deeper appreciation for the dedication, resilience, and profound impact of chaplains in fostering hope, healing, and positive change within the prison system.

CHAPTER 15

FUTURE DIRECTIONS IN PRISON CHAPLAINCY

The field of prison chaplaincy is continuously evolving, shaped by emerging challenges and opportunities. As society changes and new technologies develop, chaplains must adapt to meet the spiritual, emotional, and practical needs of inmates. This chapter explores future trends and developments in prison chaplaincy, including the integration of technology, innovative approaches to spiritual care, and the broader implications for the field.

The Integration of Technology

Technology is playing an increasingly significant role in various aspects of prison chaplaincy, offering new ways to deliver spiritual care and support.

Virtual Chaplaincy Services: The use of video conferencing and virtual platforms allows chaplains to reach inmates who may not have regular access to in-person services. This technology can provide spiritual counseling, religious education, and group support sessions, ensuring that all inmates have access to chaplaincy services regardless of their location within the prison.

Online Resources: The development of online resources, such as digital libraries of religious texts, educational videos, and interactive spiritual exercises, can enhance inmates' spiritual growth and learning. Chaplains can curate and recommend these resources, providing inmates with access to a wealth of spiritual materials.

Mobile Apps: Mobile apps designed for spiritual care and personal development can offer inmates tools for prayer, meditation, and reflection. These apps can include daily devotionals, scripture readings, and guided meditations, helping inmates maintain their spiritual practice even when chaplains are not physically present.

Electronic Communication: Secure email and messaging systems can facilitate communication between inmates and chaplains, allowing for timely and confidential support. This technology can also enable inmates to connect with family members and community resources, aiding their rehabilitation and reintegration.

Innovative Approaches to Spiritual Care

Future directions in prison chaplaincy will likely include innovative approaches to spiritual care that address the diverse needs of inmates and incorporate holistic practices.

Trauma-Informed Care: Recognizing the prevalence of trauma among inmates, chaplains are increasingly adopting trauma-informed approaches to spiritual care. This includes understanding the impact of trauma on behavior and mental health, providing compassionate and sensitive support, and creating safe spaces for healing and recovery.

Interfaith Collaboration: As prison populations become more religiously diverse, interfaith collaboration will be essential. Chaplains from different faith traditions can work together to provide inclusive spiritual care, respecting and supporting the varied beliefs and practices of inmates. This collaboration can also promote interfaith understanding and tolerance within the prison community.

Restorative Justice Programs: Restorative justice programs focus on repairing harm, promoting accountability, and facilitating reconciliation between offenders and victims. Chaplains can play a pivotal role in these programs, offering spiritual guidance, facilitating dialogues, and supporting inmates in their journey toward redemption and restitution.

Mindfulness and Meditation: Mindfulness and meditation practices are gaining recognition for their benefits in reducing stress, enhancing emotional regulation, and promoting mental well-being. Chaplains can incorporate these practices into their spiritual care programs, offering inmates tools to develop self-awareness and inner peace.

Expanding the Role of Chaplains

The role of chaplains is expanding beyond traditional religious duties to include broader support and advocacy for inmates.

Mental Health Support: Chaplains are increasingly involved in providing mental health support, working alongside mental health professionals to address the psychological needs of inmates. This includes offering counseling, facilitating support groups, and advocating for mental health services.

Reentry Planning: Chaplains play a crucial role in reentry planning, helping inmates prepare for their transition back into the community. This involves developing reentry plans, connecting inmates with community resources, and providing ongoing support to ensure successful reintegration.

Advocacy and Policy Influence: Chaplains can advocate for systemic changes within the prison system, promoting policies that support rehabilitation, restorative justice, and humane treatment of inmates. By participating in policy discussions and collaborating with advocacy organizations, chaplains can influence positive changes in the criminal justice system.

Education and Vocational Training: Chaplains can support educational and vocational training programs, recognizing the importance of these opportunities for successful reintegration. This includes facilitating access to educational resources, providing mentorship, and collaborating with educational institutions and employers.

Challenges and Opportunities

While the future of prison chaplaincy holds many promising developments, it also presents challenges that must be addressed.

Resource Constraints: Limited funding and resources can hinder the implementation of new programs and technologies. Chaplains must advocate for adequate support and seek innovative solutions, such as partnerships with community organizations and grant funding, to overcome these constraints.

Training and Professional Development: As the role of chaplains evolves, ongoing training and professional development are essential. Chaplains need access to education and training opportunities that equip them with the skills and knowledge to address emerging challenges and incorporate new approaches into their practice.

Maintaining Human Connection: While technology offers many benefits, maintaining human connection is crucial in chaplaincy. Chaplains must balance the use of technology with the need for personal interaction, ensuring that inmates receive compassionate and individualized care.

Addressing Diverse Needs: The increasing diversity of prison populations requires chaplains to develop cultural competence and adapt their approaches to meet the varied needs of inmates. This includes understanding different religious traditions, cultural backgrounds, and individual experiences.

Case Studies and Success Stories

Highlighting case studies and success stories provides insight into the innovative approaches and successful initiatives shaping the future of prison chaplaincy.

Case Study 1: Virtual Spiritual Counseling Program

Background: A prison in California implemented a virtual spiritual counseling program to ensure inmates in solitary confinement or remote facilities had access to chaplaincy services. Chaplain Laura led the initiative, using video conferencing to provide spiritual counseling, religious education, and support groups.

Success Story: The program significantly improved the well-being of inmates who previously had limited access to spiritual care. Inmates reported feeling more connected and supported, and Chaplain Laura noted positive changes in their behavior and attitudes. The success of the program led to its expansion to other facilities, demonstrating the potential of technology to enhance chaplaincy services.

Case Study 2: Trauma-Informed Spiritual Care Initiative

Background: Recognizing the high levels of trauma among inmates, Chaplain Mark developed a trauma-informed spiritual care initiative at a prison in New York. The program included specialized training for chaplains, trauma-sensitive counseling, and mindfulness practices.

Success Story: The initiative led to a significant reduction in behavioral incidents and improved mental health outcomes for participating inmates. Chaplain Mark's trauma-informed approach helped inmates process their experiences and develop healthier coping mechanisms. The program's success prompted other facilities to adopt similar approaches, highlighting the importance of addressing trauma in spiritual care.

Case Study 3: Restorative Justice and Reentry Support

Background: Chaplain Angela spearheaded a restorative justice program at a prison in Texas, focusing on facilitating victim-offender dialogues and supporting inmates in their reentry planning. The program aimed to promote accountability, healing, and successful reintegration.

Success Story: The restorative justice program resulted in positive outcomes for both inmates and victims, fostering a sense of closure and reconciliation. Inmates who participated in the program demonstrated lower recidivism rates and better reentry success. Chaplain Angela's holistic approach to rehabilitation and reintegration served as a model for other institutions.

The future of prison chaplaincy is filled with exciting possibilities and significant challenges. By integrating technology, adopting innovative approaches to spiritual care, and expanding their roles, chaplains can continue to provide essential support to inmates and their families. The case studies and success stories presented in this chapter highlight the transformative potential of these developments, underscoring the importance of adaptability, continuous learning, and advocacy in the field of prison chaplaincy. As we conclude this exploration of prison chaplaincy, we gain a deeper appreciation for the dedication, resilience, and vision required to navigate the evolving landscape of this vital ministry, ensuring that it continues to foster hope, healing, and positive change within the prison system.

CONCLUSION

SUMMARY OF KEY INSIGHTS

Throughout this book, we have explored the multifaceted role of prison chaplains and the profound impact they have on the lives of inmates. From addressing spiritual needs and providing crisis intervention to supporting rehabilitation and fostering community connections, chaplains play a vital role in the prison system. This conclusion summarizes the key insights from each chapter and reinforces the importance of chaplaincy in promoting rehabilitation and supporting inmates.

Chapter 1: Introduction

We began by highlighting the unique and challenging role of prison chaplains, emphasizing their commitment to faith, compassion, and understanding. The introduction set the stage for a comprehensive exploration of the responsibilities and experiences of chaplains within the prison system.

Chapter 2: The Role of a Prison Chaplain

This chapter detailed the various roles chaplains play, including spiritual guides, counselors, and advocates for inmates. We discussed how chaplains provide religious services, offer emotional support, and help inmates navigate the challenges of prison life.

Chapter 3: History and Evolution of Prison Chaplaincy

We traced the development of prison chaplaincy from its early roots in religious institutions to its current form within the modern prison system. Key milestones and influential figures who have shaped the field were highlighted.

Chapter 4: Training and Preparation

The training and preparation required to become a prison chaplain were examined, including theological education, pastoral training, and specialized courses on corrections and criminal justice. The importance of ongoing professional development was also emphasized.

Chapter 5: Daily Life and Duties

A day in the life of a prison chaplain was detailed, showcasing the diverse tasks and responsibilities they undertake. From conducting religious services to providing one-on-one counseling and coordinating with prison staff, chaplains engage in a wide range of activities.

Chapter 6: Addressing the Spiritual Needs of Inmates

We explored how chaplains address the diverse spiritual needs of inmates, providing inclusive spiritual care, respecting diverse beliefs, and fostering an environment of religious tolerance and understanding.

Chapter 7: Crisis Intervention and Counseling

The role of chaplains in crisis intervention and counseling was discussed, highlighting their work in providing support during crises, such as violence, mental health issues, and personal tragedies.

Chapter 8: Rehabilitation and Reintegration

We examined the programs and initiatives led by chaplains to support the rehabilitation and reintegration of inmates. These efforts help inmates develop life skills, moral values, and a sense of purpose.

Chapter 9: Collaboration with Prison Staff

Effective collaboration with prison staff, including correctional officers, administrators, and healthcare professionals, was emphasized. The dynamics of these relationships and the importance of teamwork in achieving the best outcomes for inmates were explored.

Chapter 10: Ethical and Moral Challenges

The ethical and moral challenges faced by prison chaplains were discussed, including issues of confidentiality, dual loyalty, respecting diverse beliefs, navigating power dynamics, and addressing moral distress.

Chapter 11: Case Studies and Testimonials

Real-life case studies and testimonials illustrated the transformative power of faith and spiritual support. Stories from chaplains and inmates highlighted the profound impact of chaplaincy on the lives of those they serve.

Chapter 12: The Impact of Faith on Recidivism

We reviewed evidence supporting the effectiveness of faith-based programs in reducing recidivism rates. The role of prison chaplaincy in contributing to long-term positive outcomes for inmates was explored.

Chapter 13: Community Outreach and Support

The importance of community outreach and support was emphasized, showcasing how chaplains extend their ministry beyond the prison walls to engage with communities and support the families of inmates.

Chapter 14: Personal Growth and Fulfillment

The personal rewards and challenges of the chaplaincy journey were discussed, highlighting the opportunities for personal growth, spiritual development, and the deep sense of fulfillment that comes with serving as a prison chaplain.

Chapter 15: Future Directions in Prison Chaplaincy

We explored future trends and developments in prison chaplaincy, including the integration of technology and new approaches to spiritual care. The expanding role of chaplains and the challenges and opportunities ahead were discussed.

The Vital Role of Prison Chaplains

Prison chaplains play a critical role in the criminal justice system, offering hope, support, and guidance to inmates during some of the most challenging times of their lives. Their work is essential for several reasons:

Supporting Rehabilitation: Chaplains provide spiritual and emotional support that is crucial for the rehabilitation of inmates. Through counseling, religious services, and various programs, they help inmates develop the skills, values, and mindset needed for successful reintegration into society.

Promoting Mental and Emotional Well-Being: Inmates often face significant mental and emotional challenges. Chaplains offer a compassionate presence, providing counseling and support to help inmates cope with these difficulties and improve their overall well-being.

Fostering a Positive Prison Environment: Chaplains contribute to a more humane and just prison environment. By promoting respect, tolerance, and understanding, they help create a supportive community within the prison, reducing tensions and fostering positive relationships.

Encouraging Personal Transformation: The transformative power of faith and spiritual support can lead to profound changes in inmates' lives. Chaplains play a pivotal role in facilitating these transformations, helping inmates find meaning, purpose, and hope.

Advocating for Inmates: Chaplains often advocate for the rights and needs of inmates, ensuring they receive fair treatment and access to necessary resources. Their advocacy helps address systemic issues within the prison system and promotes restorative justice.

Call for Continued Support and Recognition

The work of prison chaplains is invaluable, yet it often goes unrecognized and underappreciated. It is essential to acknowledge the vital role they play and to provide the support needed to enhance their impact. This includes:

Adequate Funding and Resources: Ensuring that chaplaincy programs are adequately funded and resourced is crucial for their effectiveness. This includes providing sufficient staff, training, and materials to support their work.

Professional Development: Ongoing professional development opportunities are essential for chaplains to stay informed about best practices and new developments in the field. Investment in their training and education enhances the quality of care they provide.

Recognition and Advocacy: Recognizing the contributions of chaplains and advocating for their role within the criminal justice system helps raise awareness of their impact. This includes acknowledging their work in policy discussions and promoting the importance of chaplaincy services.

Collaboration and Support: Encouraging collaboration between chaplains, prison staff, community organizations, and faith-based groups enhances the support network available to inmates. Building strong partnerships ensures comprehensive care and support for inmates and their families.

As we conclude this exploration of prison chaplaincy, it is clear that chaplains are an essential component of the criminal justice system. Their dedication, compassion, and resilience make a profound difference in the lives of inmates, fostering hope, healing, and positive change. By supporting and recognizing the vital role of prison chaplains, we can contribute to a more just and humane prison system, promoting rehabilitation and successful reintegration for those who need it most.

The journey of a prison chaplain is one of deep commitment and profound impact. Their work embodies the principles of compassion, justice, and hope, serving as a beacon of light within the challenging environment of the prison system. As we look to the future, let us continue to support and uplift prison chaplains, ensuring they have the resources, recognition, and collaboration needed to carry out their invaluable ministry.

APPENDICES

STUDY QUESTIONS FOR EACH CHAPTER

Chapter 1: Introduction

1. What are the unique challenges faced by prison chaplains?

2. How does the role of a prison chaplain differ from other forms of ministry?

3. In what ways can chaplains provide hope and support to inmates?

Chapter 2: The Role of a Prison Chaplain

1. Discuss the various roles that a prison chaplain plays within the prison system.

2. How do chaplains balance their responsibilities to inmates and the prison administration?

3. What skills are essential for an effective prison chaplain?

Chapter 3: History and Evolution of Prison Chaplaincy

1. Trace the history of prison chaplaincy from its early roots to its modern form.

2. What key milestones have shaped the development of prison chaplaincy?

3. How have the roles and responsibilities of chaplains evolved over time?

Chapter 4: Training and Preparation

1. What are the key components of training and preparation for prison chaplains?

2. Why is ongoing professional development important for chaplains?

3. Discuss the role of theological education in preparing chaplains for their work.

Chapter 5: Daily Life and Duties

1. Describe a typical day in the life of a prison chaplain.

2. How do chaplains address the diverse needs of inmates?

3. What challenges do chaplains face in their daily duties?

Chapter 6: Addressing the Spiritual Needs of Inmates

1. How do chaplains provide inclusive spiritual care for inmates of various religious backgrounds?

2. Discuss the importance of respecting diverse beliefs in prison chaplaincy.

3. What strategies can chaplains use to foster an environment of religious tolerance?

Chapter 7: Crisis Intervention and Counseling

1. What types of crises do prison chaplains commonly encounter?

2. How do chaplains provide support during a crisis?

3. Discuss the role of chaplains in long-term counseling and support for inmates.

Chapter 8: Rehabilitation and Reintegration

1. What are the key components of effective rehabilitation and reintegration programs?

2. How do chaplains support inmates in developing life skills and moral values?

3. Discuss the impact of chaplain-led programs on inmates' successful reintegration into society.

Chapter 9: Collaboration with Prison Staff

1. Why is collaboration with prison staff essential for effective chaplaincy?

2. How do chaplains navigate the dynamics of their relationships with correctional officers, administrators, and healthcare professionals?

3. What are some best practices for fostering teamwork and cooperation within the prison?

Chapter 10: Ethical and Moral Challenges

1. Discuss some common ethical dilemmas faced by prison chaplains.

2. How do chaplains balance confidentiality with the need to ensure safety?

3. What strategies can chaplains use to navigate dual loyalties and respect diverse beliefs?

Chapter 11: Case Studies and Testimonials

1. What insights can be gained from real-life case studies of prison chaplaincy?

2. How do personal testimonials illustrate the impact of chaplaincy on inmates' lives?

3. Discuss the transformative power of faith and spiritual support in the context of prison chaplaincy.

Chapter 12: The Impact of Faith on Recidivism

1. What evidence supports the effectiveness of faith-based programs in reducing recidivism?

2. How do prison chaplains contribute to long-term positive outcomes for inmates?

3. Discuss the role of spiritual growth and community support in preventing recidivism.

Chapter 13: Community Outreach and Support

1. Why is community outreach an essential component of prison chaplaincy?

2. How do chaplains support the families of inmates?

3. Discuss the importance of building community partnerships in enhancing support for inmates and their families.

Chapter 14: Personal Growth and Fulfillment

1. What personal rewards do prison chaplains experience in their work?

2. How do the challenges of chaplaincy contribute to personal growth and resilience?

3. Discuss strategies for maintaining emotional and spiritual well-being as a prison chaplain.

Chapter 15: Future Directions in Prison Chaplaincy

1. What future trends and developments are shaping the field of prison chaplaincy?

2. How can technology be integrated into chaplaincy services?

3. Discuss the importance of innovative approaches to spiritual care and the expanding role of chaplains.

Chapter 16: Conclusion

1. Summarize the key insights from the book on the role of prison chaplains.

2. Why is it essential to support and recognize chaplaincy as a vital component of the criminal justice system?

3. How can chaplains continue to foster hope, healing, and positive change within the prison system?

Discussion Guides for Small Groups

Guide 1: Exploring the Role of a Prison Chaplain

- Begin with an overview of the various roles a chaplain plays in the prison system.

- Discuss how chaplains balance their responsibilities to inmates and the prison administration.

- Share personal experiences or examples of effective chaplaincy.

Guide 2: Addressing Spiritual Needs and Diverse Beliefs

- Explore the challenges of providing spiritual care to inmates of diverse religious backgrounds.

- Discuss strategies for fostering an environment of religious tolerance and understanding.

- Share experiences of chaplains who have successfully navigated these challenges.

Guide 3: Crisis Intervention and Long-Term Support

- Discuss the types of crises chaplains encounter and how they provide immediate support.

- Explore the role of chaplains in offering long-term counseling and emotional support.

- Share case studies or personal stories that highlight the impact of chaplaincy during crises.

Guide 4: Rehabilitation and Reintegration

- Examine the key components of effective rehabilitation and reintegration programs.

- Discuss how chaplain-led initiatives contribute to successful reentry for inmates.

- Share success stories of inmates who have benefited from these programs.

Guide 5: Ethical and Moral Challenges in Chaplaincy

- Discuss common ethical dilemmas faced by prison chaplains and how they navigate them.

- Explore the balance between confidentiality and safety.

- Share strategies for maintaining ethical integrity and personal resilience.

Guide 6: Future Directions and Innovations in Chaplaincy

- Discuss emerging trends and developments in prison chaplaincy.

- Explore the potential of technology and innovative approaches to enhance chaplaincy services.

- Share ideas for future initiatives that could improve the effectiveness of chaplaincy.

Guide 7: Community Outreach and Support

- Discuss the importance of community outreach and support for inmates and their families.

- Explore ways to build strong community partnerships and support networks.

- Share examples of successful outreach programs and their impact.

Guide 8: Personal Growth and Fulfillment in Chaplaincy

- Discuss the personal rewards and challenges of serving as a prison chaplain.

- Explore strategies for maintaining emotional and spiritual well-being.

- Share personal reflections on the journey of chaplaincy and its impact on personal growth.

Additional Resources on Prison Chaplaincy

Books:

1. "Prison Ministry: Understanding Prison Culture Inside and Out" by Lennie Spitale

2. "The Correctional Chaplaincy: Serving the Spiritual Needs of Inmates" by Gary Friedman

3. "Prison Ministry: Hope Behind the Wall" by Dennis W. Pierce

Articles and Journals:

1. "The Role of Chaplains in the Correctional System" - Journal of Offender Rehabilitation

2. "Faith-Based Programs and Recidivism Reduction: A Review of the Literature" - Journal of Criminal Justice Research

3. "Spiritual Care in Prisons: Challenges and Opportunities" - International Journal of Prisoner Health

Online Resources:

1. The American Correctional Chaplains Association (ACCA) - www.correctionalchaplains.org

2. The International Prison Chaplains' Association (IPCA) - www.ipcaworldwide.org

3. The Prison Fellowship - www.prisonfellowship.org

Training Programs:

1. Clinical Pastoral Education (CPE) Programs - Offered by various institutions for specialized chaplaincy training.

2. The Correctional Chaplaincy Institute - Provides training and resources for prison chaplains.

3. The American Correctional Association (ACA) - Offers courses and certifications related to correctional chaplaincy.

These study questions, discussion guides, and additional resources provide a comprehensive framework for further exploration and reflection on the vital role of prison chaplaincy. By engaging with these materials, readers and small groups can deepen their understanding and appreciation of the profound impact of chaplains in the criminal justice system.

www.ingramcontent.com/pod-product-compliance
Lightning Source LLC
Chambersburg PA
CBHW072005150726
47999CB00002B/518